MOM

MOM

A CELEBRATION OF MOTHERS
FROM STORYCORPS

Edited and with an Introduction by

DAVE ISAY

The Penguin Press
New York
2010

THE PENGUIN PRESS
Published by the Penguin Group
Penguin Group (USA) Inc., 375 Hudson Street, New York, New York 10014, U.S.A. • Penguin Group
(Canada), 90 Eglinton Avenue East, Suite 700, Toronto, Ontario, Canada M4P 2Y3 (a division of
Pearson Penguin Canada Inc.) • Penguin Books Ltd, 80 Strand, London WC2R 0RL, England •
Penguin Ireland, 25 St. Stephen's Green, Dublin 2, Ireland (a division of Penguin Books Ltd) • Penguin
Books Australia Ltd, 250 Camberwell Road, Camberwell, Victoria 3124, Australia (a division of Pearson
Australia Group Pty Ltd) • Penguin Books India Pvt Ltd, 11 Community Centre, Panchsheel Park,
New Delhi – 110 017, India • Penguin Group (NZ), 67 Apollo Drive, Rosedale, North Shore 0632,
New Zealand (a division of Pearson New Zealand Ltd) • Penguin Books (South Africa) (Pty) Ltd,
24 Sturdee Avenue, Rosebank, Johannesburg 2196, South Africa

Penguin Books Ltd, Registered Offices:
80 Strand, London WC2R 0RL, England

First published in 2010 by The Penguin Press,
a member of Penguin Group (USA) Inc.

1   3   5   7   9   10   8   6   4   2

Library of Congress Cataloging-in-Publication Data
Mom : a celebration of mothers from Storycorps / edited and with an introduction by Dave Isay.
p.   cm.
ISBN 978-1-59420-261-2
1. Mothers—United States.   2. Interviews—United States.   3. StoryCorps (Project)
I. Isay, Dave.   II. StoryCorps (Project)
HQ759.M842 2010
306.874'30973—dc22   2009044752

Printed in the United States of America
Designed by Michelle McMillian

This book is dedicated to all moms honored
through StoryCorps—past, present, and future.

CONTENTS

MOM

INTRODUCTION TO
STORYCORPS

StoryCorps launched on October 23, 2003, in Grand Central Terminal in New York City. It was admittedly something of a crazy idea: put a recording booth in the middle of one of the busiest train stations in the world, then invite pairs of people to come in and interview each other about the most important moments in their lives.

But the idea worked, the project caught on, and Story-Corps has since spread swiftly across the country. In just six years, StoryCorps has recorded nearly thirty thousand interviews with more than fifty thousand participants. Determined to collect the widest possible array of American voices, we've traveled to cities, towns, and hamlets across all fifty states. Along the way, we've drawn participants from every imaginable background—every race and ethnicity, occupation, and age. Despite this amazing diversity of voices, however, the individual stories we've collected have taught us that as a nation there is so much more that we share than divides us.

Participating in StoryCorps could not be easier: You invite a loved one—a parent, a sibling, a friend, a neighbor, anyone you choose—to one of our recording sites. There, you're met by a trained facilitator, who greets you and explains the interview process. You're then brought into a quiet recording room and seated across from your interview partner, each of you in front of a microphone. The facilitator hits "record" on a pair of CD burners, and you have a forty-minute conversation. (Most people ask the sorts of questions you'll find in the "Favorite StoryCorps Questions" list at the back of the book.) At the end of the session, two CDs have been recorded. You keep one copy, and the second goes to the American Folklife Center at the Library of Congress. There, it will be preserved for generations to come, so that someday your great-great-great-grandchildren will be able to hear the voice and stories of your grandfather, your mother, your best friend—whomever you chose to honor with a StoryCorps interview.

Many participants see their session as a chance to leave a legacy. They use the time to talk about the most important people in their lives, to remember the best and worst moments they've lived through, and to pass on wisdom they've gleaned. Topics are broached that rarely get addressed in everyday conversation. It may come as no great surprise that memories of parents often feature prominently in StoryCorps recordings. Our facilitators, who have been present at each of the nearly thirty thousand interviews to date, tell us that even participants who are one hundred years old—or older—will spend time remembering (and often crying about) their mothers and fathers. Indeed, many StoryCorps conversations start with reflections on our first and often most consequential bond—with Mom.

Across the country, thousands upon thousands of people have interviewed their mothers through StoryCorps. All types of mothers have shared their stories: single moms, working moms, moms with one child, moms with a dozen or more children, mothers who adopted children, mothers who lost children, and more. These stories remind us of the unflagging hard work and singular devotion required of moms, attributes that have too often been overlooked and underappreciated. In *Mom,* we hope to do our small part to rectify this wrong.

At its heart, StoryCorps is a project about the transmission of wisdom across generations, and the stories in this book are no exception. In the pages that follow, you'll find not only wisdom, but also stories of connection and conflict, heartbreak and humor, strength and grace. I hope these extraordinary moms will inspire you with their heart, gumption, insight, and love.

Dads we'll save for another book, on another day. For now, it's time to celebrate Mom.

AUTHOR'S NOTE

The following stories were edited from transcripts of StoryCorps interviews that usually run forty minutes. We aimed to distill these interviews without altering the tone or meaning of the original sessions. At times, tense and usage were changed and a word or two was added for clarity. We did not use ellipses to indicate omitted text; in the following pages, ellipses indicate speech trailing off or a significant pause in conversation.

Words and phrases that read well are not always the strongest spoken moments, and the reverse is also the case. As a result, a story may vary slightly from audio to print.

Participants gave permission for their interviews to be published in this book, and each story was fact-checked.

WISDOM

NANCY WRIGHT, 53

talks to her son,

J. D. WRIGHT, 19

Nancy Wright: My mother, Frances Guy Ericksen, was born in Jacksonville, Florida. She was really defiant of authority. I remember a story of when she was growing up: She went into a classroom, and the screen door slammed shut behind her. The teacher thought she had slammed the door and made her go back and close it quietly a hundred times in a row—which struck her as highly unfair, since really it wasn't her problem that the door slammed. So she closed it quietly ninety-nine times, and then slammed the hell out of it the hundredth time! [*laughs*]

She got married to my dad, George Ericksen, who was probably not a very easy person to live with. They waited about five years to have me, because she wasn't sure the marriage was going to take. I remember her telling me that he proposed to her after he had fixed the toilet in the house. He came in, in his true romantic style, wiping his hands on a towel and saying, "You know, if we got married, I'd be here all the time to fix the toilet." [*laughs*] Whoo, makes you swoon! They were polar opposites. Dad was very introverted, and Mom was very extroverted. There were some rocky moments.

She had a real strong faith, and she put together prayer groups. In the early 1960s, she arranged for an interracial prayer group in Tampa, Florida. There were threats of crosses to be burnt on our yard. We were in a very conservative neighborhood, too. But that just made her even more determined to continue to do things like that.

My mom never met a stranger. She hugged people that she never met before. Her mission in life was to bring up the financial status of waiters and waitresses everywhere—she would leave a twenty-dollar tip sometimes for a five-dollar meal. And when it was pointed out to her that her tip might be a tad too high in terms of normal percentages, she was irate. There was no stopping her tipping. In fact, at the meal that we had right before her funeral we left a Frances Ericksen memorial tip for the waitress that was almost the price of fifteen of us eating there.

My mom and I were pretty compatible up to adolescence, but then we grated on each other's nerves quite a bit, and our relationship really kind of went downhill from there. Even after I left the house, I felt like all of my conversations with her were very judgment-laden and critical, especially because

I wasn't following the religious path that she wanted me to follow.

Finally, when I was about thirty, we were together at the house, and we just had a miserable weekend. I felt our relationship was awful, and I told her right before I left that I couldn't deal with her criticism anymore and that it wasn't helping me. She said, "That's what mothers do. Who would tell you if not your mother?" And I said I didn't need a mother anymore; I needed a friend. If she wanted to continue to try to be my mother that way, I didn't want it—but to call me if she wanted to be my friend.

After I left, she was very angry. I talked to my dad once in the interim, and he told me how upset she was. I almost didn't expect to hear from her, because she could be a little stubborn.

I think about two weeks after that conversation, I picked up the phone and a small voice on the other side said, "Hi, this is your friend." . . . [crying]

And it was.

Recorded in Gainesville, Florida, on October 23, 2008.

LEAH HASELEY, 43

talks to her brother,

JONATHAN SCHACHTER, 46

about their mother, Frances Fuchs Schachter.

Leah is a physician.

Leah Haseley: I have so many memories of Mom that make me smile.

I really miss her when I pick up the children from school, because she used to love picking me up from school. I remember it very clearly, coming down the ramp out of school and her having this big grin on her face because she got to pick me up. I would go running to her. My younger one still does that for me.

I remember her teaching me to drive around the neighborhood, and all of a sudden I drove up onto a curb. Mom got out of the car, giggled, and looked at the teenagers nearby and said, "She's learning to drive." I had driven completely onto the curb, and rather than yell at me, she had this positive, funny approach to it. The next time I got in the car, I drove very slowly, and I said, "I'm nervous." Rather than tell me to relax, she sat up and said, "Good. You should be nervous! This is a very dangerous thing to be doing." And to this day I still use that. I used it in the hospital a few weeks ago. I was working with a very good resident who I was training to do a procedure, and he looked up at me, and he said, "I'm nervous." I said, "Good. You should be nervous! It's a dangerous thing to do." And actually, I think that helped him relax. I think it helps to have your nervousness understood. I'm sure when I teach my children to drive, I'll miss her like crazy.

Whenever I'm having difficulty with one of the children, I often think, *What would Mom say to do in this situation?* Some of the things that Mom told me I use a lot with my kids. One is, Mom always used to say, "You be the one." *You* be the one to make up with a friend or to reach out and break the silence between you. So whenever one of the kids announces that he had a fight with another child at school and he's not talking to them, I always say, "That's not going to help you at all. *You* be the one to reach out and try to connect with your friend again." The other thing Mom used to say was, "If you're ever on the fence about whether to stay home or to go somewhere," she used to say, "just *go*!" So I say that to the kids whenever they're torturing themselves about any kind of decision that they have.

Mom took me to Boston when I was starting my residency. She was quite sick at that time, but she was bent on taking me to Boston to shepherd me through finding a place to live. It was our last trip together as mom and daughter, and we slept in the same room in this bed-and-breakfast. After we got in bed she said to me, "I want you to know a few things." And it was very clear that she wanted to give me advice before she died.

So when we were in bed, she said to me, "When you have children, always remember that a parent should be like a gas station. The children can come to you and then go out into the world and do their things and then come back for more. But be careful that the gas station stays in one place. Don't run after your children. Just stay there in the gas station to give them support." That's something that I've always governed myself by. Whenever I see myself running after one of the kids or trying to control what they're doing, I always try to stop myself and say, "I'm just the gas station."

My mother was a career woman, and she was proud of that, but I think above all she would want to be remembered as a really remarkable mother. On countless occasions she would say to me, "You and Jon are the greatest thing I ever did in my life." And I always say that to the children: "You are the greatest thing I ever did in my life!"

Recorded in New York, New York, on August 23, 2008.

WISDOM

GRACE CRUZ, 13

interviews her father,

JOSÉ CRUZ, 57

about his mother, Martha Estela Cruz Santana.

José was born in the Dominican Republic.

Grace Cruz: What was the happiest moment in your life?

José Cruz: When I heard that I was coming to New York to be with my mother. She left Santo Domingo when I was six years old. I used to see the letters that she wrote, but I wasn't a very good reader and I couldn't understand her handwriting. On one occasion, she sent a recording—I remember that it was a reel-to-reel tape. My grandmother, my grandfather, my aunt, and myself went to a neighbor's house, and we sat there listening to my mother say how much she missed us. She ended that whole recording with a hymn, "Hogar de Mis Recuerdos [Home Sweet Home]." At the end, we were all in tears.

Grace: Would you say that listening to the recording of her voice was also one of the saddest moments of your life because you hadn't been with her for so long?

José: Well, it was sad when I heard her sing and say how much she loved me, but it also felt good because I was hearing her voice, and I had never heard a recording of my mother's voice before. I think it was 1960, and we didn't have access to technology the way we do now—we didn't even have a camera, and we had just gotten a refrigerator. But to be able to listen to her voice—to me, my mother became like a movie star. So I was happy, although I did feel a yearning to be with her.

I think the saddest moment was when I saw her get on the airplane for New York City in 1957. *That* was sad. I remember that my uncle said, "You're going to cry when your mom leaves." And I said, "I'm not going to cry," because I thought he was going to make fun of me. I kept my tears inside—but I think I've been crying ever since.

For the longest time I just kept wanting to come to New York to be with her. Not that I felt lonely—I was never lonely in Santo Domingo because I had so many cousins and there was so many things to do. But I used to look at those postcards my mother would send, and I always imagined that I would either live on Fifth Avenue or in the Empire State Building— that I would live in those postcards. But when I came to New York, I was a little bit disappointed because we lived in West Harlem, and instead of living in the Empire State Building, we lived in the basement of a tenement building. But the fact that I was in New York compensated for all that—I finally was living with my mother.

One of the things that kept me going as a child is that my mother told me that I was the cutest thing in Villa Juana [a neighborhood in Santo Domingo]. She would say to me, *"Tú eres lo más lindo de Villa Juana,"* and she would give me a big kiss. I felt so good. As I grew older, I met this girl named Edwina. She said to me, "José, you're a big-headed, ugly fool!" And I said, "Edwina, you're crazy! My mother told me I was the cutest thing in Villa Juana! My mother says I'm handsome, and that's what's important to me!" She couldn't understand what I was talking about, but *I* knew. So my mother built the self-confidence in me that no one could take away.

My mother worked hard, and she told me when we first came to New York, "You know, I brought you to United States so that you could have the opportunity that I never had. I want you to take advantage of everything this country has to offer." I was in seventh grade, and I remember thinking about that and seeing her go to work, come home, cook dinner, and then leave to go to night classes to study English. And I never heard her complain: "Oh, I'm so tired! This work is so terrible!" I just saw her do what she had to do and ask me, "Have you done your homework?" So she has been, without a doubt, the most influential person in my life—in terms of work ethic, in terms of morals, in terms of just being grateful for what you have.

Grace: Based on that, are there any words of wisdom you'd like to pass along to me?

José: Well, to you I would say something that my mother told me once. She called me Chichi. She said, "Chichi, I see what other kids are doing. I don't ever want you to do anything in your life that would bring dishonor to who you are or to me." She said, "You know what I would like you to be, Chichi? Just like you've been so far: Always make me proud of you. I don't want you to be the smartest kid, I don't want you to be the best—just do the best you can, and I will always be proud of you, and I will always love you." I'll never forget that.

Recorded in New York, New York, on July 12, 2009.

VALERIE JO EGZIBHER, 62

speaks with her husband,

HAGOS EGZIBHER, 59

*Hagos's mother, Zodie, moved from Ethiopia
to the United States in 1989.*

Valerie Jo Egzibher: I learned many, many lessons from your mom. When she came over from Addis Ababa, we got to share things with her that she hadn't seen or ever been exposed to before. I'll never forget when we took her to see the singing Christmas tree—the tears were streaming down her face. I didn't know what the tears were about until after we'd left, and on the way home she said, "I didn't know God would let me live to see anything this beautiful!" That will live in my memory forever. She was just so touched by beauty of any kind.

Hagos Egzibher: I loved when your mom came to visit, too. Those were the happiest times for me, because your mom didn't understand a word my mom said, but they got along *so* *well.* They both loved cooking and they both liked children, so they just communicated by hand. They got everything they wanted done. They'd be laughing when we'd come home from work, and I'd say, "Did you have a good day?" With that beautiful smile your mother would say, "Oh, we just had a *wonderful* day today." I loved that, I *loved* that. I miss that.

Valerie Jo: I loved that, too. My mom would speak in English, and your mom would speak in Amharic, and then they'd laugh and throw their hands up. During that first visit, I said, "Mom, I don't understand how this is working." She said, "Oh, honey, I know Zodie's telling me about when Hagos was a boy, and I'm telling her about all the funny things you did. We know we're talking about how much we love our kids." They came to love each other.

Sometimes it was frustrating for me, because I would want so much to explain to your mom why something had happened or to ask more about her life. As she stayed with us, she did develop English to a certain extent so we could have superficial conversations, but we couldn't get into very many details.

We did fine in the kitchen, though. That's where I learned the most Amharic, because she taught me how to cook wonderful food, and as we would cook she would identify the names of the different vegetables and so forth. She had a wonderful way of communicating with me. Like one time her neck hurt and I gave her a neck massage, and she picked up my hand

and kissed it. Your mom brought tears to my eyes a lot, because she was so tender and so loving, and that really came through every day of her life.

I think part of what's made our life together so beautiful is the influence that our moms have on us.

Hagos: I feel the same way. We've been married for over twenty-two years. Mixing our two cultures together, we had our problems, but I think our moms helped us to get over that. I know your mom loved me because she always supported me when we had any issues, and my mom was always on your side. I remember if we argued about anything, my mom used to tell you, "He's a stone head," meaning that I'm a hardheaded person, and then she'd just laugh.

Valerie Jo: I know—she would take my side. And if you and I would get upset and I'd say anything to my mom about it on the phone, she would always say, "He's a wise man, honey. You need to listen to what he has to say." She always would say that, and she was right. That was really a smart thing for them to do, wasn't it? I mean, when I think about it, if you want to help keep things in balance, it's better to take the side of the person that is not your blood relative.

But your mom loved everybody—she was so nonjudgmental about people. I mean, whoever walked through the door, your mom was there to greet them, and she was so warm and loving with everybody, no matter what walk of life they came from. She was so gracious.

Hagos: You know, my mom was born and lived all her life in Ethiopia, and she thought she was probably going to die there. She was born in Addis Ababa and buried in Charlotte, North Carolina. To me that seems just unreal.

Recorded in Charlotte, North Carolina, on February 9, 2008.

JODY HOUSTON, 57

interviews her daughter,

BARBARA COOPER, 30

Jody Houston: You were born prematurely. The doctor came into the recovery room, and he told me that your first twenty-four hours would be very touch and go. He didn't know if you were going to make it. I couldn't wait to get into the nursery to see you. You looked like a little bird that had fallen out of the nest. You were just so fragile and looked like you needed to grow your feathers.

When you were about three months old, they sent us to Texas Children's Hospital in Houston. We were told that you had progeria and that it was a very grave situation, and to take you home and enjoy you—and that's what I've done for thirty years. They said that they would love to see you when you were a year old. When you were eighteen months old, I de-cided I'd better call them. They couldn't believe that you were still alive.

Barbara Cooper: Progeria is a genetic, premature-aging disorder. It's a rapid aging process: you skip puberty and everything else, and it's a very short life expectancy. I presented at birth with all of the characteristics, which is extremely unusual. But I don't fit all the categories—I'm tall and I don't have heart problems—and so when I was eleven, they changed the diagnosis to an unknown progeroid syndrome. I love proving doctors wrong. It's been a wild ride, but fun. I don't ever remember being sad or fearful.

Jody: You always woke up from your naps happy, and you always woke up in the morning happy. I would find myself just hoping that you'd wake up, because I knew that you were going to be happy and that we were going to have a good time.

When you were about three years old, your older sister and her friends were outside skating, and you wanted a pair of skates more than anything in the world. So we went over to Toys "R" Us, and we got you a pair of clip-on, hot pink roller skates, and we went home and put them on you. You started for the door, and I said, "No, you have to skate in the house. I don't want you to get hurt." So you learned to roller skate on deep shag carpet. You looked like a little roller-derby queen—you know, moving those arms and moving those legs, and you were content with that for a little while. And then one day you walked up to me and you put your hands on your hips, and you said, "You cannot keep me in this house forever!" That just opened up my eyes: I knew that you needed to go out there and skin your knees. So I said, "Well, that's fine. You just go out there and skate, but don't come in the house bleeding."

It was a defining moment for me when I realized that I had to let you experience life. Can you remember any of those defining moments in your life?

Barbara: Probably the most important was whenever I finally lost my vision. I miss the little things that people take for granted: just being able to glance and know what something is, like a Coke can or a gum wrapper, without having to feel for it. I'm extremely lucky that I was sighted for a long time, so I know what things look like. But I do miss rainbows and the reflections of clouds in the water and not being able to see the bobber when you go fishing.

Jody: I love it when you go shopping with me and I try on clothes, and you tell me that it looks really great. I know that you really can't see it, but it always makes me feel so good about myself. We talked the other day about how you remember your reflection in the mirror, and that you will always be young in your mind. I was so excited to hear that, because now I'll be forever young in your eyes, too!

Can you think of some of your happiest times?

Barbara: Yes, and it has to do with you. Out of all of my surgeries, you have always been there when I woke up. You're the first person I've seen, and I knew no matter what, when

I went to sleep I never had to worry because you were always going to be there holding my hand and talking to me when I woke up.

I'm very lucky to have you. You're just the best mom in the world, and I could never repay you for that. You've always taught me that we can get through it—it may not be okay, but it gets better. And that's one thing I think is definitely true: things may not be okay, but at least they'll be better.

Jody: I've always felt that when you inhale, I exhale. The closeness that we've had through all of this has been one of the most rewarding things in my life.

You call me so many times, and you'll say, "Just remember to breathe." That means so much, because I know that you know that it's been a hard day.

Barbara: And you know when I'm having a hard day, and it's just, *Breathe. Take it minute by minute.* You may not be happy that minute but—Okay, let's have a five-minute pity party, get it over with, and then let's move on. Because it's not going to do any good to keep dragging it out.

It's easier to go through life being happy than sad. If you're sad, everything is humdrum and boring. That doesn't get you anywhere. There's always someone out there that has it worse than you, so I'm like, *Well, at least I'm still moving around and enjoying things—let's just see what fun we can have!*

Jody: You know, Barbie, children aren't supposed to die before their parents do. And heaven forbid that you go before

I do. But if you did, how would you want me to remember you?

Barbara: That I did everything that I've ever wanted to do, and that you made that possible. I've enjoyed every moment with you—*every moment.* You've been my best friend.

Recorded in Abilene, Texas, on March 28, 2008.

MILLY GUBERMAN KRAVETZ, 84

talks with her daughter-in-law,

JAYNE GUBERMAN, 56

Milly Guberman Kravetz: You and I started as friends. I knew that you and my son David were going out together—you were in an off-and-on relationship. At the time, my husband was in the hospital—he became ill in September of '75 and died in January of '76. It was a hard time, needless to say. You came to visit when David was at the hospital, and then you'd also come sometimes to spend some time with me, and that's something I've never, ever forgotten. I remember walking the corridor with you. I walked beside you, sort of with my arms around my body, and it occurred to me a good bit later that what I was really doing was quite literally holding myself together. But you were there beside me. Sometimes we'd be talking about David, and if it was a period when things were kind of rocky, I would say, "Well, Jaynie, if you really love him, have patience, and it will be good in the end. Relationships are complicated at best, and you have to be patient if you want something good to come of it."

Jayne Guberman: Right from the beginning, no matter what was going on with David, I think you and I always had a really special connection. It was probably the first time I had found a woman my mother's age who was interested in the things which were really at the heart of my interests. Then, of course, we both shared a love for David. I remember saying to people that I think I probably fell in love with you before I fell in love with David.

Milly: That's a wonderful thing to hear. I think it was the fact that we could talk—I felt free to share with you. Do we want to get into how that has become complicated?

Jayne: It's kind of an unusual relationship—

Milly: It gets complicated. You and David got married, and David is my son. And I married Nate, and you're Nate's daughter. So I guess we're a good example of some kind of new math. [*laughs*]

Jayne: You met my father when David and I became engaged. You had been widowed for four years at that point, and my father had been widowed for maybe a year and a half. I don't really remember when I became aware that something was happening between the two of you.

Milly: We took a trip to Philadelphia. I remember we went to register at the desk, and there was a question of one room or two rooms for Nate and me. Your father did the registering, and I was kind of curious as to what he would say. He said, "One room," and sort of looked at you guys.

Jayne: [*laughs*] So David and I were married in August of 1980, and you were married in March of 1981. You married my father, I married your son, and it was very wonderful in lots of ways. What do you think were the best parts of that? I mean besides knowing that we would always be with you for the holidays.

Milly: I think your two daughters, Rachel and Dalia. Rachel was the one who made me a *bubbe,* a grandmother, and I'll never forget that.

Jayne: There have also been challenges—I had breast cancer when Rachel was born.

Milly: I'd be in bed with you at night while you were filling the bucket after chemotherapy, and I would empty it. It was maybe the only way I had at the time of expressing my love for you—who wants to empty a bucket of vomit? But I was grateful that I was there and able to do it.

Jayne: I don't think I could have gotten through that time without you, Milly. You have taught me so much about what it means to love someone. Over the years, especially when the girls were young, you were the person that I would most turn to when I was trying to think through how to be a mother. I don't know how many people have that kind of a relationship with their mother-in-law, but that's the way in which you were always much more than that in my life and in the lives of our kids.

Many years ago, a friend said to me, "Don't ever go to Milly with complaints about David. No matter what—no matter how much she loves you and you love her—her primary allegiance is always going to be to her son."

Milly: That does bring up the biggest issue for us, which is that we really can't speak openly about things that bother me about your father, or you about David. I think we have somehow established, without really discussing it, that those are places we just don't go. I find that very hard, because we're open about so many things. But I think we've handled it well. . . .

Jayne: I guess we have, because we're still here.

Milly: When I introduce you, I say, "This is my daughter-in-law," and then I kind of grin and say, "She's also my step-daughter . . . but mostly, she's my friend." That's how I've always felt.

Recorded in Boston, Massachusetts, on October 20, 2006.

SUSAN LISKER, 53

talks with her daughters,

ELIZABETH LISKER, 21
and MADELYN LISKER, 13

Susan Lisker: Our family formed in just a magical way. I had had several miscarriages, and I wasn't able to carry a child. I used to say I didn't care if a bird dropped it off on my doorstep, I just wanted to be a mom. And when you came along, Elizabeth, we literally adopted you and closed on your case the next day.

I was very concerned about discrimination with you and then when we adopted Pete—you're both Korean—and in the beginning there was a lot of it. Now there are so many children that are adopted from other countries—you see that pretty much everywhere you go. But twenty-one years ago it was not as common for Caucasian families to have Asian children, and some very disparaging remarks were made to us. We were at a hot-dog stand once, and a man came up to us and said, "I guess they'll send anything from China these days." People would just be very forward with questions. On the grocery line, someone once said to me, "Is your husband Japanese?"

Madelyn, you were a total surprise. We were married twenty years—I was forty years old—and I found out that I was pregnant with you. We kept it to ourselves for a very long time, because we just assumed that I would miscarry as I had done previously, and lo and behold, there you were! By the time Madelyn came along, I was a fairly experienced mom, and one of the first questions a relative said was, "How does it feel now to have one of your own?" I was so taken aback by that— I was still in the hospital, Madelyn was all of six hours old, and my thought was: *I already have two others of my own. What are you asking me?* Maybe it was that post-birth fog or something, but I really couldn't get what they were asking. In the middle of the night, I was holding Madelyn and it came to me. I said, *Oh my gosh! What kind of dumb question was that?*

There were people who commented that Pete and Elizabeth and Madelyn weren't really siblings because they had different biological parents, and we'd always say, "Of course they're siblings. When one hugs the other, do they feel love for each other? Of course they do. If one has a fight with the other and pushes them around and they fall down, does it hurt? Yes, it does. Well, it's the same no matter where they were born—they're growing up in the same house, they're being loved by the same parents, and they are as much brother and sisters as anybody else." So I was always very protective.

A lot of people asked if it felt different to parent an

adopted child versus a biological child, but it was your personalities that made the relationship different, not the fact that you were adopted or biological. You're just three very different people.

Elizabeth Lisker: I remember when you sat Peter and I on the couch and you said that you had a surprise for us, you and Dad, and that you were going to have a baby. To be perfectly honest with you, I was quite upset, because I liked having the attention. Knowing that the baby was a girl, in my head—I mean, I was in the second grade—I thought I should be the only girl in the family.

Susan: I remember when Dad and I told you, you cried for three hours the first night and a little bit for the next several nights afterwards. One of the things that you had said to me was that you thought there was no way we could love you as much as we would "a child that grew in my body"—those were the words that you used. Do you remember any of that?

Elizabeth: I don't remember, but when you're growing up and you know that you're adopted, and you go to school with kids that have biological parents, you just get in the mindset that children that come from their biological parents are—they're different, like in the way that their parents treat them, or that they love them more. I had the mind-set that you loved us the most because that's all you knew, and that having a baby might change that. [*laughs*] It hasn't changed. I'm still loved exactly the same if not more, I'd like to think.

Susan: Well, there's more to love about you as you grow.

When you were five years old, you had your birthday party at Chuck E. Cheese. That night, when we were tucking you into bed, you were telling me about what you liked about your day and what you didn't like about your day. You asked me if I thought your birth mother was thinking about you on your birthday. I remember saying to you that I thought that she would always think about you on your birthday. And you asked me if I thought that she knew you had your birthday party at Chuck E. Cheese. I remember saying that I didn't think they had Chuck E. Cheese in Korea, but I'm sure she knew that you had a really wonderful birthday.

Do you still think about your birth family?

Elizabeth: I would like to go visit Korea and see what it's all about, but I have no interest in meeting my birth mother— I'm perfectly fine with the mother that I have.

Susan: Madelyn, it's your turn. You're growing up in a family where both your brother and sister are adopted. When you were about four years old you were fighting with your brother, and you shouted at him, "I grew in Mommy's stomach and you didn't!" I had to stop the fight and say, "But all of you grew in my heart." You didn't like that at all, because you thought that you had a definite advantage by having been born of our flesh. So what's it like to be the only biological child in the family?

Madelyn Lisker: The biggest thing I've noticed is that Liz and Pete have their airplane day—that's the day when they came to our family. The only day I came to the family was my birthday. I only have one day of the year, and they get two. Otherwise, I think it's just like nothing anymore.

If I could make a wish, it would be to make the age gap smaller, because I have a friend who's two years apart from her two brothers and they're a lot closer. When I was little, I felt like Liz and Pete were always talking and I wasn't really included in that.

Susan: At the dinner table, when you were very small, they would be talking about their day. You were about three years old and in preschool, and you'd sit at the edge of your high chair and you'd say, "Today at school . . ." And everybody would just keep talking and ignore you. You'd go a second time: *"Today at school . . ."* And we'd still keep talking and everybody would ignore you. Finally, you would lift up as far as the high chair would let you, and you'd shout out, "TODAY AT SCHOOL, GUYS!!!" Everybody would stop and look at you, and your brother would say to you, "All right, Madelyn, what is it?" And you'd sit there and say, "Now I can't remember." That would happen night after night after night.

Elizabeth: We're all different people in our own ways— and I'm not just saying that; we are actually *very* different people. Our personalities clash sometimes, but at the end of the day, we're just a family that loves each other.

Susan: That's very true. Elizabeth, I loved you from the

moment I saw your picture. And Madelyn, I loved you from the first moment also. I love you both and your brother very much today, too, but for different reasons than in the beginning. I really love who you're turning out to be: really good people.

Recorded in Buffalo, New York, on August 12, 2008.

ROSELYN PAYNE EPPS, 78

talks with her daughter,

ROSELYN ELIZABETH EPPS, 47

Both women practice medicine in Washington, D.C.

Roselyn Payne Epps: I always knew I'd have a career and children. It's interesting, you hear a lot of people talk about "Which can I have—one or the other?" Why not both? Coming from a family of African-American people the women have traditionally worked—so it has never been a big mystery about "either-or," just how you balance it.

I never let my children think anything was more important than they were, but I never let anyone at work think that anything was more important than my job. I never talked about my kids at work . . .

Roselyn Elizabeth Epps: . . . And you didn't bring work home.

Roselyn Payne: Nope, I left my work there. You make adjustments. I can recall when you all were starting school and I was working in a clinic. I was the only pediatrician there, so

I had to be there every day. If anything happened at home that would keep me from being there, there may have been fifteen, twenty, forty parents bringing their children for examinations who would be disappointed. So I knew I had an obligation to be at work. But I also knew I had an obligation to my children.

You all were very responsible. For instance, I would tell you, "Tell me in advance when you're going to have a program. Ask the teacher: 'When is the recital going to be?' Don't tell me on Monday to come to a program on Friday— you've been rehearsing and rehearsing and rehearsing for months!" So then I had the opportunity to get someone to substitute for me. It was a partnership between us.

Roselyn Elizabeth: Well, as far as partnership was concerned, we all had our responsibilities. There were specific chores—there were days everybody was supposed to do dishes. If we were going to entertain, somebody was supposed to sweep, somebody else cleaned the walls, and somebody else pulled the weeds. I was the "A-One Sweeper." You and Dad were very creative with your names: "Oh, you're the best wall washer!" "Oh, boy, you really know how to pull weeds!" Only later we realized, *Boy, we were bamboozled into our chores!* But we were sweeping, and we were so happy.

Roselyn Payne: That was your name—the "A-One Sweeper."

Roselyn Elizabeth: We all knew what our jobs were and what our responsibilities were: you were the parents and we were the kids. It wasn't a time where people were friends and buddies; that wasn't our generation at all. You weren't smothering—I guess the new term is "helicopter parents." Sometimes you don't want your parent there every second to experience it and video it. Although you never missed a school play, never missed a parents' night, never missed *anything*. For four children!

Roselyn Payne: I would get there sometimes, and I would be one of two parents. I used to say, "Where are the people? Where are the parents?"

In the early days, your dad had evening office hours and he'd be late getting home. So we made a decision to sit down as a family and have dinner at six thirty—*every night*—no matter what. When you went off to college or medical school or wherever you were, you all knew if you called home at six thirty, you could talk to the rest of the family because that was *our time*. And if your dad had to go back to the hospital at night, didn't matter. He came home and we had dinner together every night, and we had breakfast together every morning. We had two meals together every day.

Roselyn Elizabeth: Did your experiences in medicine affect being a mother and vice versa?

Roselyn Payne: One thing I learned is that *all* parents want their children to succeed, and *all* children want to succeed. I used to go to talk to sixth graders, and I'd say, "What do you want to be when you grow up?" I never heard a child say, "I want to be a drug dealer." I never heard a child say, "I want to stand on a corner." But somewhere in between, something happened.

I think being a mother helped parents respect me. I would give them advice, maybe about feeding an infant. I was young then—you know, I finished medical school in my early twenties, and I guess I looked younger than that. I would tell them, "You don't have to think about feeding the baby every moment," or whatever it was. And they would look at me like, *Well, what do you know about that? She doesn't know what's going on!* And I'd say, "I have four children." Oh! That gave them new respect: *Well, maybe she knows what she's talking about!*

Looking back, people will say, "Oh, you were a pioneer—there were only five women in your class!" But I didn't see it. I was following my dream to be a pediatrician and have a family.

You all have done very well. But I take no credit and I take no blame. People say, "Aren't you proud?" My mother always said, "Don't be proud; just be thankful." So when you were coming along, I said, "I won't take credit because I'm not going to take blame either!"

We never encouraged you particularly to go into medicine. When our oldest son was about twelve, he said that he thought he would go to law school. So we said, "Why are you going to go into law?" He said, "Doctors work too hard!" At the time, he had a very good friend named Bruce whose father was a lawyer, and Bruce said he was going to go into medicine. "Ask Bruce why he wants to go into medicine when his father's a lawyer." He did, and Bruce said, "Lawyers work too hard!" So I said, "The truth of the matter is, you work hard if you're successful—no matter what you do. So you have to decide to do something you enjoy, because you're going to work hard." So he said, "In that case, I'll go into medicine." [*laughs*]

Roselyn Elizabeth: Well, of course you're my one and only mother, and it has evolved towards friendship also. A lot of people laugh and say, "You all act like sisters!"

Roselyn Payne: True. We are very close, and we're a lot alike. We're buddies. We talk every day, all day long. Your dad sometimes says, "What are you all laughing about so much?"

I love you very much, and I'm very pleased with who you are. As I've said, I'm not proud; I'm thankful.

Recorded in Washington, D.C., on July 10, 2009.

ARLENE FREIMAN, 58

talks to her daughter,

LESLEY FREIMAN, 26

Arlene Freiman: I wanted children from the time I can remember. It just wasn't as easy to have children as I expected.

Dad and I got married when we were really young: I was twenty, and he was twenty-two. If it had been up to me, I would have had a baby right away, but we were still in school and we had a lot of school to go. So we waited to have a baby. When I made the decision to go to law school, one of the considerations was whether I wanted to wait another three years for children. After I did wait three more years, it wasn't so easy to have children.

Your older brother, Michael, was my sixth pregnancy: there were five miscarriages before him. I was despondent. I just felt that this was the most important thing to me, and it wasn't happening. I couldn't look at babies, because it just reminded me that I didn't have one. I avoided people who were friends when they started to have children. It wasn't a good strategy, but it was the only way that I knew to handle it at the time, and they were such wonderful friends that they let me do that.

After law school I worked for an attorney named Jim Beasley for ten years, and I was having this series of miscarriages, and he knew it. When my sister Wendy had Richard, Jim came into my office, and he sat me down on the couch. He said, "This is your nephew—you can't avoid this baby. This is really important, Arlene." Through it all, Jim always said, "This will happen for you. You'll have children."

When I was pregnant with Michael, I did what I did for all of the others—I didn't tell anybody, and I didn't really want to admit to myself that I was pregnant. There was this feeling that maybe I could protect myself, that if it didn't work then maybe I wouldn't be as unhappy. But it doesn't work like that. When you deny yourself joy, it doesn't make the pain any less if it doesn't work out.

But when I got past the first three months, I began to believe that I might really have a baby. Well, I *say* that I believed it, but really I didn't. When they were taking me from the labor room to the delivery room, they said to me, "We see the baby's head." I looked at Dad; he would never tell me something that wasn't true. I said to him, "Is there really a baby there?" And he said, "Yes." So I thought, *Maybe there is really a baby there!* I know that when I was in the delivery room, I was stunned.

Giving birth to a baby is a tumultuous experience, and I think that there's a lot of excitement and a lot of fear that surrounds it. But I don't think I felt any of the fear. I was so thrilled to be there—I was just *so* thrilled to be there. Without a doubt, it was the high point of my life. It wasn't just with Michael—it was all three times. When I delivered you it was equally the high point of my life, and also with Dan.

Lesley Freiman: It's funny, 'cause hearing about it from other people, I just get such a different experience about what it's like giving birth to a child.

Arlene: I look back on these almost fifty-nine years, and there's one sentence that was the best thing that anyone's ever said to me: I was in the delivery room with Michael, and there was a resident on call who looked at me and said, "Within an hour, you're going to be a mommy." Every time I think of it, I just think, *What a gift!* It just rings in my head all the time.

Lesley: Do you think it's affected your being a mom that it took so long?

Arlene: I know for sure that it made me much more patient as a mother. Because there are times that really do try your patience. But I don't think that I would have raised you another way if it hadn't been so difficult. Maybe it helps to remind me that every day of my life I am so grateful to be the mother of wonderful children. The one thing that I wished for in my life happened to me. I'm just forever grateful. . . .

My old boss Jim Beasley died a few years ago, and they

named the law school at Temple University after him. Last spring Dan invited me to go with him to the Admitted Students Day, and we walked up the steps to the law school, and I saw the name: the James E. Beasley School of Law. I looked at Dan as we walked up—Dan didn't know that Jim had always said to me, "This will happen for you"—and I couldn't believe that there I was, walking up the steps of the Beasley School of Law with my youngest son. It was remarkable to me.

Lesley: So why did you want to talk to me about these things?

Arlene: It's like your bat mitzvah: there's a time when it becomes really important to express the feelings that I have for you. It was important for me to do that today, when I thought that I had the opportunity.

Lesley: I hope you know that you express this much better than you think you do. We all really know that. You tell us every day in one way or another.

Recorded in Philadelphia, Pennsylvania, on November 21, 2007.

JOHNELLA LAROSE, 50

speaks with her daughter,

KASIMA KINLICHIINII, 22

Johnella LaRose: I had two children and I was three months pregnant with you, Kasima, when your dad left. And I remember thinking, *Now what am I going to do?* We were living in the Los Padres National Forest [California] with other Indian people, taking care of horses and cows. We got $436 a month on welfare, and I did beadwork, I sewed, I did laundry, I ironed—I did everything.

Kasima Kinlichiinii: You would pick up cans, too, and I was like, *Oh my God, here she goes again, picking up cans!* The other day, my cousin was drinking ginger ale, and I said, "Don't you throw that can away!" And I was like, *Oh, God, I sound like my mother!* [*laughs*]

Johnella: When you were four and the boys were ten and twelve, I just couldn't make it anymore. I was in the Native

American Health Center in Oakland, and one of the gals gave me a flyer about a pre-apprenticeship program in the trades. I had no idea what that was, but I thought, *I've got to do something.* So I went through the apprenticeship, and I became a union cabinetmaker.

My first week my paycheck was $240, and that first year I made $13,000 in the shop—at that point I had been getting $8,000 a year on welfare. The next year I made $19,000, the year after that I think I made $26,000, and it's gone up from there. So it changed *everything.* It was a lot of money—hard-earned money. I didn't think I was going to make it—I was the only woman in a cabinet shop with twenty-nine guys—but I did it. I was running the shaper, the planer, table saws—everything.

Kasima: And you'd never used any of those before?

Johnella: Never—but I learned. One time I brought a cabinet home, and I set it on the kitchen table. Your brother walked in, and he goes, "Where'd you buy that?" I said, "Your mother made it!"

Kasima: I remember you just being busy, busy all the time. You were always dirty. [*laughs*] Dirt in your nails all the time. I didn't really understand what was going on, but I'm really thankful that you did that for us.

Johnella: Do you remember—I didn't have a car, so I had to ride my bicycle to drop you off at the babysitter's at five thirty in the morning. Then I rode three miles to work every single day for two years. I was in really good shape! And one day it was raining, and you said, "No more bicycle! No more bicycle!" I mean, you were just *sobbing*. I thought, *Okay. Maybe we should try and get a car. . . .* [*laughs*]

There were problems, no doubt. This one guy would say to me, "Why are you here? You should go home." He didn't think women belonged in the shop. I was like, *You got to be kidding me, right?* I said, "I don't have a husband to take care of me. I'm feeding everybody in this house. There's nobody paying my bills."

I *had* to survive: I had kids to take care of. And I had nothing else—I just squeaked through high school, had kids when I was really young—so I had to hang in there. And I did. If you can get to the job, you can do the job. Sometimes the rest of your life can stop you, and that's where you have to just say: *No matter what happens from three thirty in the afternoon to seven o'clock the next morning, I just have to deal with that so I can get back into that shop.* And that's what I did. I was proud of that—I *am* proud of that.

I go to places now and I see reception counters that I helped build, and I'm just proud that I did it, you know? Now I'm going to college for the first time—today was actually my first day—and I know now that I can probably learn anything. But I didn't know that before.

Kasima: I just had a baby; he's four and a half months old. You make me motivated to support myself and my son. I'm not exactly sure what I want to do yet or how I'm going to do it, but I'm going to do *something*. I'm just wondering how I can be a good mother to him by myself.

Johnella: I think that the creator puts something in front of you, and you just have to grab it and see what you can do with it.

Kasima: I hope I can be as strong as you are.

Johnella: You *are* as strong as I am.

Kasima: Do you have any words of wisdom for me?

Johnella: As a parent you can make a lot of mistakes, but you can always fix them. If you say something that you didn't mean, just say: "I didn't mean that; I was upset." Just fix it right away, because people carry things inside and you don't want that. You'll make mistakes—you're a human being. So just forgive yourself and move on.

I know there've been days when I raced home and tried to get dinner on the table, and somebody's lost their bus pass, someone's done this, someone's done that—none of that matters. What really matters is that you keep your cool with your children. The house being clean—forget it, it doesn't matter. Having dinner on the table—it doesn't matter. If you're stuck and it's raining out and you're in the car, have a picnic in the car. I know this for a fact: it'll mean more to your child than rushing home, screaming at them, and trying to get dinner on. The baby can be in his car seat and you can sit in the backseat with him, and you'll just have a beautiful time that he'll remember forever.

Kasima: Thanks *a lot* for being my mother.

Johnella: You're welcome. I just wanted to make life better for you kids. I know that there's only so far I can go. Now it's up to you to take it and run.

Recorded in Oakland, California, on August 18, 2009.

DIANE GAYLES, 58

talks with her daughter,

JENNIFER GAYLES, 30

Diane Gayles: When I was in Buffalo in kindergarten through third grade, I was a very good student. Unfortunately, when we moved to Lancaster, a suburb of Buffalo, the course work was much more rigorous, and so I didn't do as well initially. There was quite a lot of civil-rights activity at the time, and it was very difficult being the only black children in a white neighborhood. But it taught me a lot.

I was going into fourth grade—it was my first day of class, and the teacher's name was Ms. Devaney. She was calling names and having everyone line their desks up according to her chart. As she was calling off the different children's names, they were helping each other move their desks and put them in the different rows. Then when she called my name, no one came to help me. So I had to struggle to move my desk by myself. The teacher said, "Won't someone help Diane?" And no one would, so she came and she helped me move my desk. That was my first introduction to racism.

I was all alone and I knew I was all alone, and quite honestly, my father had told us that that was probably what would happen. But there was brightness there as well. This is back when you had recess and you actually went out on the playground and played. Everyone was out there playing, and I just knew no one was going to talk to me. I was standing there watching the boys—they were playing, roughhousing and kicking a ball, and the girls were on the swings and they were chatting away. So I just stood next to the building by myself. And then this one girl in our class came up. Every time I think about it, it makes me cry . . . Melissa Tousley. I'll never forget her. She came up to me, and she said, "Would you like to play with me?" [*crying*]

I never felt so alone. But she came and offered friendship to me when no one else did or would. She'll never know how much that meant to me. Unfortunately, when we got to junior high her family moved away, and I don't know where she went. I've always thought about her. She has no idea what she did for me. . . .

Jennifer Gayles: . . . I never knew that story.

Diane: Your father chose your name, but I wanted to name you Melissa because of Melissa Tousley.

Jennifer: What was going through your mind when you first saw me?

Diane: I couldn't believe it. First of all, I couldn't believe that I had a daughter. Because I had all brothers, I felt that I would always have boys. First, your brother came along, and then when you came along, I said, "It's going to be another boy." So when you were born, I just started thinking about all the things that we were going to do and how I was going to dress you up. I had lots of plans for you—still do.

You were just wonderful; you were a piece of cake. Taking care of you was easy because you just took care of yourself! I remember one instance when I had to take your brother to the bus stop. George was five years old, and you were two. We lived about five houses from the corner, and I had to stand on the corner with George, waiting for the bus. So I said, "Jennifer, stay here in the crib—don't get out," and I left you in the house and took George down to the bus stop. We had been doing this for quite some time, no problem whatsoever. Well this one particular day I'm standing at the bus stop and I'm looking at the house, and I see the curtains move, and I go, "Why are the curtains moving?" I could just see them moving, and I said, "Oh my gosh!" I knew you had gotten out of the crib, and I didn't know what you were going to do. So I grabbed George and I ran back to the house—the bus was going to come any moment. I got in the house, and I said, "Jennifer, why are you out of your crib?" And you said, "Mommy, the phone was ringing."

Jennifer: I didn't want you to miss a call!

Diane: I guess not—you were a telephone operator at a young age. So I put you back in the crib and told you not to worry about the phone. I actually took the phone off the hook and then took George back out, and we caught the bus.

But you were a very easy child. You were just a little clingy. You weren't my daughter—you were my shadow. When you were four, I said to your dad, "She has to go to nursery school. I can't take it! Anywhere I go, she's right behind me!" So we scrimped and saved and lived on beans and rice, and we got the money together to send you to nursery school. That was the best thing that ever happened for you *and* for me. I wound up with peace of mind, and you made friends. When you came back you started telling me about your adventures at nursery school, and then you went off and played by yourself—

Jennifer: I wasn't your shadow anymore. That was the beginning of my independence.

Diane: Hallelujah!

Jennifer: Do you remember when I left home for good?

Diane: You were funny because you came home from college and you said, "I'm only going to stay here about three, maybe four months, and then I'm gone." I really didn't think that would happen, but it did. At first the house was *so* empty. That first week—I'll never forget it—it was so, *so* empty. I came home and I just walked from one bedroom to the other, and I was just feeling so depressed. That lasted about a week.

Then I realized how free we were. Oh, Martin Luther King, *Free at last, free at last!* And that's when our life really took off. I can remember you and George calling and leaving messages: "Where are you two now?" We were gone all the time.

I am so proud of you and your brother, of the way that you have turned out. Your dad and I are *so* proud of you. You may not know that, or maybe you do—but it always helps to say it.

Recorded in Buffalo, New York, on August 15, 2008.

GABRIELLE HALL, 29

talks with her sister,

DANIELLE HALL, 27

about their mother, Martha Hall.

Gabrielle Hall: Mom was amazing. I think she was the coolest person, because she did so many things and was really good at all of them. I picture Mom on the beach in Maine. I picture her with the auburn hair that's short, not the gray hair.

Danielle Hall: I see her lying in the bed that Dad made, with the sunshine coming in, looking over the water. That was really my favorite time to go in—we would lie down on the bed and just kind of fuss or talk. That was always our time with her.

She taught me things about relationships that I still use. She told me that when you fight, you have to decide how much it really matters to you. If it's not worth getting upset about, let it go. And if it is worth getting upset about, you have to be brave enough to bring it up with the other person.

And if you *aren't* brave enough to do that, you have to let it go. Once you've discussed it, it's over and you never bring it up again. That, I think, is just the *best* advice I've ever gotten.

I keep remembering the night of the eclipse—it really crystallized for me what I loved about Mom. It was the night before I went on my first date with Brian, and I was really high-strung and worried. I was at home getting ready, and she was trying to calm me down. There was going to be a lunar eclipse, so we turned off the lights, and we put our feet up on the windowsill. We were trying to look at the eclipse, but neither of us had our glasses, so we couldn't really see anything. The lights were off, and we were just totally giddy. Mom got out a roll of Neccos and handed them to me, and I was sniffing each one in the dark, trying to sniff the colors that she liked to eat.

It wasn't the big conversations with Mom that mattered; it was just being able to spend time together and be ourselves.

Gabrielle: She was such a fighter—we knew for fourteen years that she had cancer and that she was dying, but she believed at the essence of her that she was not going to die.

Danielle: I feel blessed that we had fourteen years. Before she died, I told her that I thought that she had been a wonderful mother, that she taught us how to be strong and independent and smart and capable of doing anything, that I loved her, and that we would be okay. But she really wanted to know that *you* would be okay.

Gabrielle: I always imagined that I would just die after Mom died. I couldn't even fathom how my life would go on without her. I think the most shocking thing was just waking up and realizing I was still breathing and deciding to go on.

In the end she went so quickly. We just got into this state of her being chronically sick. I remember taking her to chemotherapy and talking to her in the chemo room, and she was just so sick, she was *so sick*. I would be like, "Mom, you don't have to keep doing it." And then it came true. She was back in the hospital again, they had done some tests, and they said, "It's fourteen days." And then she died—fourteen days later.

Danielle: I remember our last Thanksgiving, with Mom in her pajamas.

Gabrielle: The day she finally came out of the hospital was Thanksgiving. We had always had the same Thanksgiving, but this year's Thanksgiving was different. Then it started being a *really* significant day, that we really had stuff to be thankful about—that we had Mom. It was the last meal she had. Mom died on December 5th.

At her service we asked everybody to wear red shoes, but we didn't really explain why. Mom would wear red shoes to chemotherapy, and she'd tell everybody there that you couldn't have a bad day if you were wearing red shoes. So I got up and I said that everybody was wearing red shoes because Mom believed that you couldn't have a bad day when you were wearing red shoes. I had on a pair of red high heels, and I'm wearing red clogs today.

Danielle: I like the idea of going out on December 5 and putting on red shoes and just celebrating.

Gabrielle: We're going to use days like Thanksgiving and days where we wear red shoes to remember her. She lived life so fully, and we can't ever forget to do that.

Recorded in San Francisco, California, on November 23, 2005.

DANIELLE HALL (*left*) AND
GABRIELLE HALL (*right*)

FANNI VICTORIA GREEN-LEMONS, 49

speaks with her daughter,

DANYEALAH GREEN-LEMONS, 15

about her mother, Pauline Green.

Fanni Victoria Green-Lemons: When I was your age, my mother and I had to negotiate about letting go. She and my dad had raised us to be fiercely independent, magnanimously hopeful, and well grounded—with common sense and a wonderful sense of the presence of the Lord in our lives. But actually providing opportunities for us to go out into the world and be those things was scary for her, I think, and so we had bouts and battles and skirmishes. For such a long period of time, my mother and I seemed to communicate across a great divide of misunderstanding, and I want so much not to have that with you.

Danyealah Green-Lemons: We always talk about your relationship with Nana, and I think my relationship with you is *a lot* different. We talk about things, and I come to you when I need help or when I need to talk. I keep learning from you every single day—simple things, like how to be a strong and independent woman, how to live life, and how to treat people—that's a big one because you treat people wonderfully and you give *so much*. You keep in touch with people. I'm definitely learning from you how to maintain relationships.

When I see you with Nana, I'm always observing how you communicate with her: your body language and what you say and how you say it to her. When she talks, I see that you are listening but that you are also analyzing what she's saying, so that when you say something, it will make sense to her even though she might not agree with you.

Fanni: When she got older, my mom was so very feisty about her level of care. She would not let us—her daughters— help her, and I was angry. I thought she raised us to do exactly that, and she wouldn't let us do it. I was afraid that we weren't going to be able to be of help to her until she got to the place where it was clear that she wasn't going to be able to help herself.

I will never forget asking my mom to see assisted-living facilities. She would say she would go one day, and then she wouldn't go the next. We just didn't know what was going to happen. And so I called the mother of my best friend, and I said, "What do I do?" And she said, "Fanni, mothers can never resist their children when their children simply bare their hearts. So don't go in and try to be strong for your mom. Don't go in and try to make her *do* anything. Just look your mom in the eye and tell her you need her help in order for you to help her." So I did. And my mom looked back at me and said, "I will go. Although I'm *so* scared, I will go." And I put my head in her lap, and I cried. But she didn't. She put her hand under her chin like she does, and she just looked off to the side. Then when I got done crying, she said, "Well, we'd better go do this before I change my mind."

What I want to say to you is that sometimes life catches you by surprise and you feel unequipped to handle what it brings you, but every bit of life you've lived before that moment equips you to live through it. That's what I would give to you.

Recorded in Tampa, Florida, on December 11, 2008.

DEVOTION

PAM PISNER, 54, AND DAN PISNER, 55

talk to their daughter,

SHIRA PISNER, 25

Pam Pisner: Dad and I had known each other for five years before we got married, and then it was actually eight years before you were born. We talked about having children because we thought it would be really cool to see the product of the two of us. We were such a good team together, and we just wanted to know what it would be like to make some babies.

Shira Pisner: How did the product come out?

Pam: Beautiful. We love the product. It was a little bit more of a product than we originally planned on. [*laughs*] But it was good.

Dan Pisner: We thought that we most likely wouldn't have children—

Pam: Well, we were afraid, because I had such a difficult time conceiving—and that was pretty devastating. I think we started trying seriously maybe two or three years after we got married. And then it was a few years before we decided to take Pergonal, which is the fertility drug that I took to get pregnant. It was something that we had said we would never do.

There were a lot of risks—not just the large chance of multiple births, but there were other risks, too. We said we wouldn't go that far, but when it got down to *Okay, if we want to have children, we've got to do this,* we decided that we wanted them bad enough that we were going to give it a try.

Dan: Mom-Mom, Pam's grandma, prayed and prayed that Pam would get pregnant—she thinks she may have prayed too hard.

Pam: If we ever write a book, that's going to be the title: *I Think I Prayed Too Hard.*

Of course when I first found out I was pregnant, we were elated—we couldn't believe it. It actually happened on the second round of Pergonal, which was good for a number of reasons. One is, it happened. Also, Pergonal is very expensive and not covered by insurance.

One of the first things we did was buy a little Nissan Stanza, because it would be a family car and with the hatchback, we'd be able to put the stroller in the back and carry all the little things we'd need for our little baby.

Dan: We got delivery of the Nissan Stanza about a week before Mom went in and got the sonogram. After that, the Stanza was worthless.

Pam: At eleven weeks, I had gone in for a sonogram at the radiologist's office—Dad was in the waiting room. The first radiologist came, did the ultrasound, and then walked away. Then another person came in with him, and they sort of talked to each other and they left . . . and then a *third* person. I was trying to ask what was going on, but they weren't saying anything. So I started to get a little nervous, and probably by the fourth or the fifth person, I wanted them to let Dad come in, but they weren't letting him. I saw them pointing to the screen like they were counting to five. So finally, Dan, you came back, and I went, "It's a litter."

And you said, "What are you talking about?"

And I said, "There are five babies."

Dan: I said, "What are you *talking* about?"

Pam: They wouldn't tell us anything; they needed to have the doctor tell us. So we went back to Dr. Grodin's office, and he was a well-known fertility specialist. He had an office with this huge desk that was up high, and you sat down low in these little chairs. So you feel little and he's *big*.

Dan: It was like being before God.

Pam: So we went in, and we're sitting in those little chairs and a few minutes later he walks in and he's looking a little green around the gills. I just looked up and went, "It's five babies, isn't it?" He just shook his head, because he'd been teasing us all along that the largest multiples that he'd had in his practice was triplets—just one set of triplets. Everyone else had been twins.

Dan: Back when you guys were conceived there was nothing called selective reduction; it just wasn't practiced at all. And so when Dr. Grodin said, "We see at least five embryos," his question to us was whether or not you want to have five kids.

Pam: The options were all or nothing.

Dan: You've got to understand, we had two weeks to decide, and our questions were: number one, *How dangerous is it for Mom to carry five babies?* and number two, *What were the chances of even having one viable baby? What are the chances they could all be very unhealthy? Either they don't survive or they're very unhealthy all their lives?* So we thought about all of that in those two weeks.

Pam: I think we were extremely apprehensive because it was such a high-risk pregnancy. I mean, we knew you were going to be premature, but we didn't know how premature. So it was very scary. We thought, *What are we going to do with five babies?* One is hard enough, especially never having done this before. And you can't exactly go to your next-door neighbors for advice.

Dan: Yeah, "When you had *your* quintuplets, what'd *you* do?"

Pam: And even people with twins—it's a totally different thing. But we agreed that we were a good team, and we have a strong, solid relationship. Having a baby puts a strain on a relationship, and having multiple babies puts more of a strain on a relationship. We knew ours was strong and together we could do it.

We went to see Bubbe and Pop-Pop, my mom and dad. We were just coming from the doctor's office. I mean, I was terrified; I was in tears. They tried to soothe us, but they were upset and worried like we were. And then we went to see Grandma and Pop-Pop, Dad's mom and dad, whose reaction was, "Oh, wow! One baby is a joy—so this is five times the joy!"

So we went back to Dr. Grodin, and I think he saw that we were leaning toward continuing the pregnancy. He said if anybody could do it, I could: I had everything going for me that could be going for me. We learned much later on that the other doctors in his practice pulled him aside and told him he was out of his mind—that he should have just told us right off the bat that we should have aborted the whole pregnancy—

Dan: Because they knew this is a high, high, high, high risk. At that time, I think there were eight recorded sets of quintuplets *ever* that survived.

Pam: We didn't come home all at once with five babies. After you were born we'd been told by the hospital that we'd have a staggered homecoming because you were different weights and had different health issues that needed to be overcome before you would be able to go home from the hospital. As it turned out, we got two babies home on July 28 and two more babies on July 29. Then Elliot stayed an additional five weeks.

Dan: When everybody was home and nobody was sleeping through the night yet, two of you guys were on one feeding schedule, and two others were on another feeding schedule—because we got two one day, two the next day. And then Elliot, five weeks later, he was on the third feeding schedule. If you do the math, we were feeding babies twenty-one out of twenty-four hours a day. And we didn't want to bottle-prop because we thought it was very important to hold each and every one of you, each time you were being fed. That meant we never, *ever* slept.

Pam: And then Dad stayed home from work for the first year.

Dan: Mom had been working at the Food and Drug Administration since she was seventeen years old, and she had a good career. She was making more money than I was, and we figured it made sense that I'd stay home. So that's why Mom went back to work and I stayed home for the first year. But I had huge amounts of help because Bubbe had set up a volunteer group. Anyone who said they were willing to come by and feed, she'd schedule them: "You'll be here Wednesdays at two o'clock to four o'clock and feed these babies." She had it all scheduled.

Shira: So Mom, how was it when you first went back to work?

Pam: Well, on the one hand, I kind of felt like I was missing out. You always worry that you're going to miss the firsts—

but you know, if I didn't see the first step that you took, I still saw the first step that *I* saw that you took, and that was just as special. On the other hand, I think I benefited from it. Because I honestly looked forward to coming home and being with you every day. It was really, honest-to-goodness quality time.

Dan: We wouldn't answer the phones, we wouldn't see people, we wouldn't do *anything*. It was just you guys, Mom, and I.

Pam: I think I enjoyed it more because I had that break during the day where I was doing other things besides taking care of babies—because when we were with you it was *intense*. It was all babies: there was no time for anything else.

Dan: But you kids were *so* much fun. You were always, *always* laughing, always giggling, always something going on.

Pam: We loved the activity. We still do. The house is always full, and people come and go. One of our fears when we first found out was, *How do you love five babies all at once?* We wanted to make sure everybody got equal attention. But it was not a problem.

When you were infants it was a little hard because you'd be feeding a baby and then you'd want to sit and cuddle and just have a little bit of quiet, one-on-one time. You'd want to contemplate their fingers and toes, and we couldn't do that when there were four other infants. When you got older, then we were able to break it down a little. Even just a trip to the grocery store—whoever went to the store would take one or two. And even that half hour of one-on-one time was special.

So we would try to do things like that to the extent that we could. When you got even older, you would go and spend the night at Bubbe and Pop-Pop's. Maybe two or three of you would go, and we would keep the rest at home. It was just amazing if one baby was gone, how much easier it was.

Shira: If you could do it over, would you have done the same thing?

Dan: In a heartbeat! I know Mom agrees with this too. You're our kids—I mean, that's a given. But you're our best friends, honest to God. We would rather be with you all than pretty much anybody else. And that's about you guys, because I don't think a lot of parents say that about their kids. It's a reflection of our children.

Shira: Well, you guys give us all the credit, but really we turned out the way we did because of you, because of how you raised us.

Dan: We don't see it that way. We think you raised *us*— you outnumber us!

Shira: Thank you for all you've done. [*laughs*] I don't know how you did it.

Pam: Before we had children, it was just the two of us. We were married for eight years, and we were busy. I mean, every night of the week we were doing something. I don't know what we were doing, but we were never home. And then after you babies were born we were *very* busy, but we weren't doing *any* of those other things, and in fact could not even *remember* what those things were. But it wasn't important to us. What was important to us now was just being with you guys. Those other things must have just been time fillers—because this is the real deal!

Recorded in Olney, Maryland, on April 19, 2009.

SARA GLINES, 61

talks with her husband,

GREG GLINES, 62

Sara Glines: I grew up on a farm in Randolph, New Hampshire, which is a very small town. My family's been there for seven generations, and our kids are the eighth generation. I grew up in the house where my dad was born. Our closest neighbors were almost half a mile away.

I got pregnant when I was sixteen, and nobody knew. I kept it a secret from my parents and my sisters, and I didn't tell anybody at school—nobody knew except for the father. I had just lost a bunch of weight, so I didn't *look* pregnant— I just looked like I was putting my weight back on. I knew I was going to break my parents' heart, so I didn't want to tell them. I thought, *Maybe I'll miscarry.* Of course, that didn't happen.

I stayed home from school the day I went into labor. My parents took me to the hospital, thinking it was appendicitis, and when I got there, of course, it was not. When my parents told my younger sister, who was away at school, that I had just had a baby and that she was an aunt, she said, "Well, if you think *that's* bad, she smokes, too!" [*laughs*] And I think my dad was far more upset with the fact that I smoked than I had just had a kid!

I had Mark a month after I turned seventeen. The father's name was Bruce, and his mother was dead set against us getting married. That was pretty traumatic. I can remember sitting in the living room at the farm, and it was myself and Bruce, his mother, my mother, and their priest—they were Catholic, we were not—telling me what a bad person I was for ruining his life. His mother refused to sign the consent forms for us to marry. A good friend of my parents was a minister in a Congregational church, and he found a state where you can get married without parental consent if you are the father of a child. So when Mark was two months old, Bruce and I went down to Dover, Delaware, and we got married. The marriage didn't last, as one would expect. We stayed married legally I think five years; we were actually together about three.

Having Mark was exceedingly difficult, life altering, and a blessing at the same time. He was just a wonderful, wonderful baby—he's been wonderful all through his life. From time to time people have asked me, "Would you do it again?" And my answer has been, [*crying*] "As long as I could have the son I have, *yes!*"

I decided that as a single mom, I needed to do something other than working as a waitress—so I decided on mechanical drafting at the community college in Berlin. Actually, I was the first female to go through the college's mechanical drafting curriculum, and I just found engineering fantastic. I ended up being the first female to be hired in the paper mill in a technical position.

You and I met in the community college, when Mark was nine. We were living together a while when we told him that we were getting married. He said, "That's great! I always wanted a dad—now I can have help taking care of mom!"

Greg Glines: And then son number two has another story to tell. . . .

Sara: We talked about having another child. The three of us sat down, and you and I said, "We're thinking about having another child." And Mark said, "That's great—I never wanted to be an only child." So I said to the both of you, "So all three of us are going to bring this child up?" "Yep, that's fine." And I'm thinking to myself, *Right*. But anyway, we went through the pregnancy, and I continued to work at the paper mill.

I remember one day I wasn't feeling all that great, and I drove myself home. It was about noon. I called you at maybe three o'clock and said, "I think you better get home." I was obviously in labor, but it wasn't a big deal—my water had not broken. It was March 15, the Ides of March. We were traveling to the hospital, and the road was full of frost heaves. We hit a frost heave, and my water broke. I'm thinking, *I'll never make it to the hospital*. But I didn't dare tell you.

Greg: We had a Ford Fiesta, and you had kind of pushed the seat back a little bit. You started taking your pants down, and I said, "Sally, *what are you doing?*" And you said, "The baby's coming!" And I said, "No, it's not."

Sara: But I was right! So at that point you're steering the car to the side of the road, and you reached down and you caught Kevin before he hit the floor of the car while I reached over and pulled on the emergency brake so we wouldn't roll down the hill—team effort! Then I asked, "So what are you going to do now?" And you said, "Well, I'm going to call an ambulance." I checked his eyes and his nose and his mouth, and he was doing just fine. It was really chilly, and I lifted up my tunic and put him against my body so that he could have as much body heat as possible.

You ran to a nearby hotel to call an ambulance, and I asked you to get towels. You came back with the towels, and I wrapped Kevin up in those as best I could—

Greg: Our friend at the hotel had explained to me that calling an ambulance was not the way to do it—she said, "Drive your ass up to the hospital! *Right now!*"

Sara: So you started doing that. And it was really neat because it was about five o'clock, and as we're driving to the hospital I'm waving to all the people who I work with because they were on their way home. So we get to the hospital, and the emergency room doc got in on the driver's side. I just rolled Kevin over, and they clamped the cord and cut it. They took Kevin in, and then they took me.

When we got into the hospital and got everything all settled, the birth certificate came. I looked at it, and for place of birth it said, "En Route." I said, "I'm not signing it." They said, "Well, you have to." I said, "No, I do not. I know where he was born, and he was born in Randolph." So I called the capital in Concord, and the little gal there said, "Oh, Mrs. Glines, you're going to have to sign it." And I said, "Oh, no I'm not! Let me talk to your boss." So I talked to him, and I said, "Are you telling me that if I had gotten out of the car and laid on the ground covered with snow, his birthplace would be Randolph?" And he said, "Yes." Well, that did it—there was no way I was signing that birth certificate until it was changed. And it was—to "En Route, Randolph, New Hampshire."

Recorded in Berlin, New Hampshire, on June 14, 2009.

TIA CASCIATO SMALLWOOD, 58
talks with her daughter,
CHRISTINE SMALLWOOD, 27

Tia Casciato Smallwood: When we were in high school, my friends and I would talk about being teachers. But when I went to college, I decided to major in economics, and I started taking finance and accounting courses. I had this great professor—this wizened, just *miserable* old man at Rutgers. I had him for first-year accounting, and I was the only woman in the class. When I showed up in second-year accounting and business law, he said to me, "Miss Casciato, you are the only woman that has ever gotten this far in my class, and I will make sure every day is a living hell for you."

He used to grade us on our class participation and how we would answer questions, and he said to me at the beginning of every class, "I hope you prepared, Miss Casciato, because the most difficult question of the period will be yours." I had to fight to even enroll in these classes. I said, *This is crazy,* and I really became very much of a feminist.

In my senior year, I couldn't get a job interview. I think I wrote eighty letters. I remember saying to my dad, "I don't know what I'm going to do if I don't have a job." He said, "Well, you went through your savings, so I guess you either have to live on the street or you'll have to come back home."

Finally, I got an interview at Johnson & Johnson. I owned one dress: it was a minidress in shades of red and pink with these big block geometric squares. And I had tights and heels on. My hair was really long, no makeup, and I was thin. I walked in, and this guy interviewed me for fifteen minutes. Then he said, "You need stand up and turn around." I said, "What are you talking about?" He said, "Stand up and turn around." I stood up and I leaned over his desk and I said, "I don't need this job *that* much." And that's when he said, "You're hired!"

They offered me this job for $7,020 a year, $135 a week. I called my father and I was crying: "You know, Dad, there are guys from Rutgers who are getting offers at J&J doing the same kind of work I am for $11,000 to $12,000, and they're going to pay me $7,000." And he said, "It's a really good company. You are really good, and you need to know that somebody will recognize that. You should take the job." I did, but I remember being really, really insulted. That was the way it was, and I think you know my feeling: I think it's like that today, only it's much more subtle.

Steven was born in 1978. When I got pregnant, I went to tell my boss, and he couldn't believe that I was going to have a baby. I said, "Don't worry about it; I'll be back." And he said,

"I don't know what we're going to do about your stock options." I said, "What do you mean?" He said, "I don't think that we know what to do when you're on maternity leave." Then I got this phone call from HR, and they said, "We don't know what to do about stopping and starting your options." I remember saying, "I cannot believe that you guys are going to worry about six weeks!"

A couple of days later I got a phone call from the chairman, who I knew because I had been one of his direct reports. He said, "Hey, Tia, first of all, you should have told me you were pregnant. Secondly, congratulations. Third, don't worry about your options." He said, "HR has to write a policy now because I'm sure there will be other women who go on maternity leave." I couldn't believe that I was the first one. It was 1978, not 1878!

I think that if I had any regrets in my life, I regret that Daddy and I didn't understand how hard it was going to be to raise kids and work at the same time. I really had this idea that I could do everything 100 percent—like you can be 100 percent worker, 100 percent mother, and 100 percent wife. And you can't. It's impossible. I traveled all the time. I worked long hours. And it was just burning me out. I didn't know what was going on with you guys. I didn't feel as connected as I wanted to be. So finally, when you guys were seven and five, I said, *That's it. There's got to be a better way*.

Christine Smallwood: Did you ever have moments where you felt like you regretted leaving work?

Tia: No. I never felt that way. I loved just being with you guys. I mean—this is where I'm going to start to cry—as much as I learned about politics and about work and about myself, I don't think I learned how to be a real human being until I was with my children and suffered with them and watched what they go through. You would give anything for them. You would give up your life, your career, and your home. You unconditionally love them, and I think that is what made my life complete. So no, I never regretted it.

I just want to put on the record how absolutely delighted I am with you as a human being. I mean, you're just a wonderful person. You're compassionate, smart, and insightful, and you are just absolutely delightful to be around.

Christine: I always strive to be more like you—it's true.

Tia: Keep on being who you are.

Recorded in New York, New York, on February 2, 2008.

WANDA ZOELLER, 56

talks to her partner,

SUSAN HERNDON, 51

about her mother, Ethel Zoeller.

Wanda Zoeller: I was the last of six children. I was born in Clarksville, Indiana, at a very small hospital. I was actually delivered in the area where little boys are circumcised, because they didn't have any space left in any rooms. They shoved my mom off into another room where they kept the clean laundry and circumcised little boys.

I lived a good portion of my growing up—until I was thirteen—in the projects of Louisville. Today it's considered kind of a rough area, but when we were growing up everybody knew each other and took care of each other.

We had an area in the back of the projects where we'd take our garbage. They'd cut trees, and there'd be piles of trees back there, so some of us kids would go back there and make forts out of these tree branches and such. One time I was back there trying to find stuff to make our fort, and I found a nest. I didn't know these little, tiny, naked animals were rats. So I took off my tennis shoe, picked them all up, and put them in my shoe. I ran home, very proud of the fact that I had a bunch of little animals. When I showed them to my mom, she totally freaked out, took my shoe, and threw it in the garbage. Of course she was freaking out that I was handling these rats, and of course I was freaking out because she was throwing away these little, bitty pets into the garbage! She wouldn't let me have my shoe back. [*laughs*]

My mother always kept a nice house, always kept us together. I never knew we were very poor, and I attribute that to her. I can remember times sitting in the dark, and of course, as kids, it was a game for us. We had a choice between food and utilities, and of course we picked food. When we were growing up, my dad would always add to the grocery list "lightbulbs and toilet paper." Mom would never get the lightbulbs or the toilet paper, because we'd have to get food instead. So it kind of became a joke: If we wanted a lamp in the bedroom, we'd take this lightbulb out of the living room and carry it to the bedroom to use. We might have had one or two lightbulbs that moved around the whole house.

And then sometimes if we ran out of toilet paper you'd have to use newspaper or whatever was handy. This sounds kind of crude, but we'd have to rough up the paper and then use it for toilet paper. So I always said when I got older, if I didn't have anything else, I was always going to have toilet paper. I told you that story, and now to this day, you always make sure our cupboard is full of toilet paper. So I always joke and say, "I'm displaying my wealth," because I'm showing everybody how much toilet paper I have.

I think I had the greatest mom in the world. She was very forgiving, nonjudgmental, would give you *anything*. People say they'll give you the shirt off their back—but, I mean, she literally would. She never hit us or whipped us, although trust me, there were times I wish she would have just spanked me instead of sitting down and telling me that she was "disappointed with my actions." It would be easier for her just to whip me and put me in a room, but she didn't do that. She sat down and taught us that there's consequences to everything you do, and if you can live with those consequences, then go ahead and make those decisions, but before you make those decisions, try to think them through. I think the most important thing she gave to us was to care for people, to be generous, and not to be judgmental. She was a huge influence in my life. I had a lot of opportunity to go very bad in my life. Thank God I had my mother to help me focus on doing the right things and not to screw my life up to the point of no return.

When Mom died, I was blessed to be with her. The whole family was with her, as obviously you were, Sue. I was lying in the bed next to her, holding her, and telling her it was okay to let go, because I knew it was probably hard for her to let go of us. So we had to make sure she knew we were going to be okay. That was probably the proudest, the happiest, and the saddest moment of my life. I could only hope that I could be as lucky—just surrounded by the people you love, holding you while you take your last breath. And the very last thing she said to us was that she loved us.

Recorded in Louisville, Kentucky, on October 14, 2007.

WANDA ZOELLER (*left*) AND
SUSAN HERNDON (*right*)

JERRY JOHNSON, 52

interviews his mother,

CARRIE CONLEY, 80

Jerry Johnson: Now, Daddy left when I was around five or six. You had six kids at that point. And I guess the thing that puzzles me, as a parent now, is how you kept all that together. You know I cannot remember one Christmas that I didn't feel like I was the luckiest kid in the world, even though now I realize we had hardly anything in terms of money. How did you hold that together?

Carrie Conley: I worked at Outer Drive Hospital in Detroit, and we got one sick day a month: that was twelve days a year. If I was sick, I would still go to work. I would never call in a sick day—I was saving those days for Christmas. And at Christmastime, they would pay me for those days. That's what I would use for y'all's Christmas. They had a nice Salvation Army. Around the first of December, all the rich people would clear out their children's toy chests, and they would take all these nice toys to the Salvation Army. I would go there and I would get me a huge box, and I would go around and pick out toys. I would get that whole big box of toys for a couple of dollars. Then I would get y'all one new toy, because that's all I could afford. Then I would use the rest of the money for food. And so it always seemed like we had a big Christmas.

Jerry: I remember those boxes of fresh oranges and apples and the cakes—

Carrie: I baked homemade cakes, and I still do that today. So we just had a nice Christmas, because that's what I'd worked for. I'd say, "Jerry, write three things down that you want." I would pick one so you'd have one new toy. I never did tell you it was Santa Claus, though, 'cause I said, *I cannot give no man credit for this.*

Jerry: I told that to some of the kids at school once. We were talking about Santa Claus, and I said, "Man, hard as my mother works, we weren't gonna give no white man the credit!" [*laughs*]

You've been through a lot. What would you say, thinking down through the years, would be some of the things that you were the most proud of?

Carrie: You know the thing that I'm most proud of? That I was able to raise my six children and you all turned out as well as you did. Because that was really a load on my shoulders. And you know, the Lord blessed all of them. Just like when you were a boy: I asked you what you wanted to be, and you said you wanted to be a doctor. So when you graduated out of medical school, Washington University, that was the happiest day of my life—when you walked across that stage and you became a doctor.

I took you to church, and I took you to Sunday school. I took you when you wanted to go, and I took you when you didn't. But son, it paid off—you have to agree.

Jerry: Oh, I agree, I agree.

Carrie: I'm so grateful how the Lord blessed me, and how my children turned out. Whatever you attempt to do, don't give up; you just got to press on, and God'll make a way.

Recorded in Detroit, Michigan, on May 26, 2007.

DENNIS MCLAUGHLIN, 58

interviews his mother,

THERESA MCLAUGHLIN, 82

Dennis McLaughlin: When I was born, what did the doctors say to you?

Theresa McLaughlin: They said that you had a long road ahead of you. At six or eight months, you had surgery on your spine to see what was causing the paralysis in the lower part of your body. They discovered that you had a vertebra and a half missing in your spine, and it had gnawed away the nerves that controlled the lower half of your body. They said that you would need a lot of surgery and a lot of time in the hospital, but they said, "From the neck up he's just fine; if he wants to do something, at least give him the chance to try to do it." And that's always the way that I've felt. You've tried a lot of things, and you've always been successful at everything that you've tried.

Your grandfather McLaughlin was quite handy with building things, and he built you a little wheelchair when you were very small. He built it out of wood that he had, and the wheels are from—I'm not sure if it was a bicycle or a tricycle—but it was all stuff that he had around. I think you were one year old, and you got around in that very, very well.

Dennis: I spent a lot of time in the Shriners Hospital in Springfield, Massachusetts. A few years ago, we drove through Springfield. It suddenly dawned on me what an incredibly long trip that was—and we were on interstate highways. I thought, *Well, in 1948 most of these roads didn't exist.* So what did you have to do to come and see me?

Theresa: We could only visit on Saturday. The hours were from eight in the morning until four in the afternoon—no exceptions. For quite a while, your dad and I used to go by car. Then your dad and I separated, and I didn't have a car. So I had to take the bus to Springfield. I had to work at the time, and we were living with my parents. So I would get out of work at midnight and take a bus to Portland, and then from Portland to Boston. Then when I got to Boston I had a two-hour wait for the bus to Springfield, and I was afraid to go even out of the station, so I'd wait right in the station for two hours until the bus came.

The hospital was on the outskirts, so when I got to Springfield I had to take another bus from the city to the hospital. But I couldn't go and see you until eight o'clock in the morning, and so I'd wait at the station until I knew that I could get into the hospital to see you. I'd spend the whole day with you. At four o'clock on the dot everybody had to leave, even though a lot of us traveled very far. One little boy in your ward lived in Canada, and his parents could only come once in a great while, but when they came they had to leave at four o'clock just like the rest of us.

It was very difficult leaving you, because the minute you'd see me putting on my coat or getting ready to leave, you'd start to cry . . . and then I'd hear you crying all the way down the hall. So that was very difficult, but every minute that I spent with you was well worth it.

Dennis: When I was fourteen my legs were amputated. Up until that point there wasn't much that I couldn't do. And then when that happened—this sounds strange—but it was a very liberating experience because my legs were sedentary: they were just there; I couldn't use them. I worked well around them—but then without them, it was almost like there were literally no limits at all.

Theresa: Well, you had wonderful doctors, and when the doctors told me the best thing for you, even though it sounded cruel, would be to amputate your legs, it was very difficult. But one doctor told me, "Dennis will roll with the best of them after he has his legs amputated"—and you always have.

Dennis: A particularly hard time I remember was when they said, "Well, now that you no longer have your legs, you have to go away and be rehabilitated." I remember being furious about that. I asked them, "Why?" and they said, "Everything is different. You have to relearn all these things." It made no sense to me whatsoever because up until that point I had adapted to everything.

Theresa: Well, I didn't feel that you needed to go and learn everything all over again, and I told the doctors that. They said, "He really has to go. And for the first couple of weeks you shouldn't come and see him, because he'll be very homesick and he'll want to go home." So I took you. It wasn't easy to leave you, because I knew that you knew everything that they were going to teach you. About two weeks later I got a telephone call. I said, "Oh, he's homesick?" And they said, "Oh, no! On the contrary, he's keeping this place alive. But he already knows everything that we've tried to teach him," which we tried to tell them in the first place, "so you can come and get him." It didn't take me long. When I got there, I said to the receptionist, "I came to get Dennis." She said, "If you can find him—he's all over the place."

So you came home, and you've always been very independent and capable of doing everything. One day you came home from work at the watch shop in Portland, and you said, "I'll be home late tomorrow." I'd never ask questions because I knew when you said something, you had a reason for it. This went on for quite a while: about twice a week you'd get home late, and I thought, *I wonder what he's up to?* One day you came home and you said, "Ma, I can swim." I said, "You can swim?" You said, "Yeah, I've been going to the Y, and the instructor there told me if I came at a certain time on certain days that he would teach me to swim all by myself in the pool."

People always treated you like you were no different from anybody else: the kids let you play football; you were the pitcher on the softball team. They let you do everything that they did. I remember one instance where you and the neighborhood kids were on the back porch. The window was open, and I could hear you talking about, "What are you going to be when you get big?" One was going to be a policeman; someone else was gonna be a fireman. When it got to you, somebody said, "What are you gonna do, Dennis?" You said, "I'm goin' in the army." And one of your friends said, "You dummy, you can't go in the army—you can't march!" You said, "No, but I can ride in a jeep!" [*laughs*]

So, that's the attitude you had all the time. I'm not just saying this. A lot of people that I know—even today—will say, "Boy, he can do just about anything, can't he?" And I say, "Yes, he can—and he always could."

Dennis: I have a son now, and he's two years old. When he looks at me, he just sees his papa. And we were talking about the fact that when he gets older, he's going to have a really great attitude because he will accept people very easily. He won't see them for the fact that they're in a wheelchair or that they walk with a cane or crutches.

Theresa: And of course having a new grandson—

sometimes it's more than I can take. I'm just so happy—it actually makes me feel younger. My blood pressure has gone down a lot, and the nurse said, "What are you doing different?" And I said, "Well, I don't think I'm doing anything different." And she said, "I know what it is—it's your new grandson!"

Dennis: I guess that it's just kind of the luck of the draw. Some people aren't so lucky, and some people are very, very fortunate. And I'm one of them.

Theresa: You've been a wonderful son. I couldn't ask for any better.

Recorded in Portland, Maine, on September 17, 2006.

RAY MARTINEZ, 56

Ray Martinez: I was raised in the Colorado State Children's Home in Denver. They kept kids from infancy to age eighteen or nineteen years old. I was there from infancy to age five.

I remember that the orphanage had this practice where they would allow potential parents to check you out like a library book: they could borrow you for a couple of weeks, take you home, and see if you were a fit for their family. A couple of times I remember riding in the car, leaving the orphanage with potential parents, and them just trying to make me happy and make me laugh, and me sitting in the front in these little booster seats cars had back then in the fifties. But I never remember being at their homes. What I do remember is getting returned to the orphanage, riding back in the backseat of the car with no one talking to me. So I sensed right then and there that for some reason or another they didn't like me. I couldn't put it into words; I just felt it. I can distinctly remember riding up to the orphanage, which had an oval road in the front, and always feeling like I was back home. When I got out of the car, I can remember a couple of times running in the orphanage saying to myself, *I never want to leave this place again!* And I think that was a lesson that I carried with me in law enforcement and as mayor—that I believe that you should accept everybody for who they are and reject nobody.

The second lesson was how you share things, because in the orphanage you really didn't own anything—nothing was yours; everything you had was shared. If it was cold outside, they'd bring out a table of coats and everyone threw on a coat, and every day you had a different coat when you went outside to play. You didn't know anything about Santa Claus because they never brought Santa Claus to the orphanage. They would bring military people who would hand you gifts, and you'd take turns opening your gifts. You'd put them in the center of the room, and then everybody could play with all the toys. So I had more than just one toy; I had hundreds of them—you just shared everything that you had.

Finally, I was adopted. I was five years old. The matron sat me on the front counter, and my dad looked at me and my mom looked at me, and I looked at them—we just kind of stared at each other. My dad shoved this blue stocking cap over my head, and my mom shoved this little toy stuffed dog in my arm. They swept me off the counter, and away we went.

My mother said, "We never brought you home on a trial basis because they told us, 'We think Ray is experiencing rejection.'" So they came for several weeks just to observe me. They were enamored with me, I guess, and they said, "That's who we want." They picked me up and they never took me back.

So here I was with the first two things I ever owned in my life—the stocking cap and the toy dog—and off to home I went. I didn't have a suitcase—there was nothing else to take but the clothes on my back. They took me to my new home on Sycamore Street, and they said, "This is your home." I looked at it and I thought, *Okay, whatever that is.* They took me to my bedroom and said, "This is your bedroom, this is your toy box, this is your closet, and everything is yours." This was all kind of confusing to me. They put me in my bed, which looked like a giant bed. It was just a single bed, but back in the orphanage you slept on small cots. And then they closed the door and shut the lights out. Well, I wasn't used to that. I was used to sleeping in a room full of kids and the matron walking down the hallway checking up on you every hour—I used to watch her come down the hallway and hear her heels clicking. I was used to all this noise and raucousness and people around, and all of a sudden it was dead silent.

As my mother remembered, "Within the hour, you jumped out of bed, came to our room, and jumped in bed with us and slept with us for the night." They suddenly realized, *He's not used to being alone.* So they let me stay for the night with them. Then the next morning was interesting, because that's when they tried to explain to me that we're your mom and your dad. I just kind of looked at them like, *What's that?* I didn't understand.

My adoptive mother died in 1994, on Easter night, and my adoptive dad died in 2000, on Father's Day night. I loved them dearly—they live in my heart just like they're alive today. They taught me so much and cared for me so much. When my mother passed away, I went through her cedar chest and I found my stocking cap and the toy dog that they gave me—the very first things I ever owned. Each year, I keep them under the Christmas tree as a reminder of where I came from. I never knew my mother held on to those things, and I'm very thankful to her for hanging on to me.

In April of 2005, I filed for my records from the orphanage. Six months later I received a big package with microfiche film of all my adoption records, but they redacted everything about my biological mother's identity, her name, and my biological father's name.

There was a two-page document, and at the very top edge of that second page, where it overlapped with the first page, they had forgotten to white out my biological mother's name. So I had her name, and I thought, *I've got a lead here,* and the search was on.

All of a sudden, *bam!* I had an address, and I had a phone number. I had this feeling: *My gosh. I am so close, so quick.* I started the search in October, and November second I was making the phone call. When I first made that call, my heart was racing. I thought, *Well, she has to be elderly at this point.* And I felt, *I don't want to scare her. I don't want to turn her world upside down.*

All these things were racing through my mind. *What am I going to say?* Then she answered the telephone, and I said, "I'm looking for a Gloria Quintana. You may not be the right one." I was trying to give her wiggle room in case she decided she didn't want any part of this. I asked if she was born down in the San Luis area, and she said she was. So I started conveying the story that I was doing a genealogy search and I was trying to see if she was part of my family or not. So she was answering a few questions, and I told her that I was born in Grand Junction and relinquished to an orphanage. When I got to the point, she hung up the telephone.

Persistent as I am, I called right back, and she hung up the telephone again. So I thought, *Well, she's persistent like me: she <u>must</u> be my mother.* I ended up calling again that evening. She answered the phone, and I said, "Gloria, this is Ray. Don't hang up. I just wanted to share a couple of things with you." I said, "I want to thank you for giving me life." She listened, and I kind of reviewed what my life was like: being adopted from the orphanage by my parents and becoming a shoeshine boy and always having the dream of being mayor someday. I used to shine the mayor's shoes, and I used to tell myself, *One of these days I'm going to wear those shoes.*

She listened intently, and then she told me, "Well, I have your numbers, and if I want to pursue this I'll let you know." I told her I wouldn't bother her; I'd wait for her to call me— she had my promise. I got to thinking after I hung up, *My gosh, it could be years from now.*

Well, the next morning, my cell phone rings, and it's her. She said, "This is your mother." I thought, *Wow.* She said, "Look, son, I want to tell you everything that happened. I think you have a right to know, because you're my son."

She explained that she had given birth to me when she was about twenty years old. She was violated against her will, and they didn't know what to do with me. She knew she couldn't afford to raise me. During that phone conversation, she broke down and cried several times. You could tell this really hurt. But I think she felt good about being able to say it.

After we talked for about thirty minutes on the telephone, she said, "I want to meet you." We agreed to meet on a Monday, at IHOP, at nine-thirty in the morning. I thought, *I'm going to get there at nine o'clock and watch her walk in.* I wanted to see it all. Well, when I walked into the restaurant at nine o'clock in the morning, she was already there—we both were thinking the same thing. I looked at her sitting across the restaurant, and I thought, *Boy, she does kind of look like me, if that's her.* I looked at her and she looked at me, and I kind of pantomimed with my mouth, "Are you . . . ?" And she shook her head yes, and so we knew that was it. We hugged each other, and she looked at me, and she said, "Well, thank goodness, you don't look like your father!" I had been worried that I might have the same appearance as her attacker, and I was hoping that I didn't. So we had the same thoughts of getting there early and what was the first worry on our mind.

We had a marathon breakfast, and she proceeded to tell me even more details of the story. I found why she was so frightened when I called and why she hung up. She told me, "You know, it was a hard birth, and when I signed the relinquishment papers, I had told the doctor, 'I just want to hold him one more time.'" She said he looked at her kind of strange, and he told her, "You know, he died."

So she was left to believe that I was no longer alive all these years. But she said, "For some reason or another, I knew you were alive, and I don't know why. There was no evidence of that—I'd been told everything to the contrary. Sometimes, over the years, we'd go to different orphanages just to look and see: What if we saw him? What if we found him by chance?"

When we left the restaurant that day, we held each other, and I said, "Just think—you waited fifty-four years to hold me one more time."

Recorded in Fort Collins, Colorado, on April 23, 2008.

ANNETTE ZUMBA, 54

talks to her sister,

JENEVIEVE ZUMBA, 46

Annette Zumba: Mom had seven children before she was twenty-eight; I'm the oldest and you're sixth. Now that you have two very active children in your home, how do you look at the job Mom did?

Jenevieve Zumba: I get stunned daily at how she *ever* was able to do the laundry. [*laughs*] Seriously, I'm just completely stunned at how she gave us each our own time. On our birthdays, we had the choice to have dinner alone with Mom and Dad or with the six brothers and sisters. I always chose to be alone with Mom and Dad—and I remember that quiet time between us.

I think that she raised us really kindly and also filled with joy. I remember, even when we were poor—we got very poor after Mom and Dad split—we went to the movies once a month. No matter what, Mom would pay for all of us to go to the movies for a double show and any food we wanted: hot dogs, popcorn, sodas, whatever. It didn't matter how poor we were—on food stamps or whatever, it didn't matter—that was our treat once a month, and we could rely on that.

Mom taught us always to watch out for each other, that love comes first, that you don't ever say, "I hate you." You say, "I hate it *when you do* such and such." She always told us to remember the good things that we loved about each other. Even though we were so scattered during the day, we all came home and had meals together. If you were not home by six o'clock, someone was looking for you.

Annette: I remember Mother's Day: We were very young, and she took us to a park. Everybody's pushing each other, and we're all laughing, and it's very, very fun. She asked us to please call her Mrs. Zumba on Mother's Day. So we would be swinging in the swings and say, "Mrs. Zumba, can you push me?" "Mrs. Zumba, look what Rick is doing to me." *Mrs. Zumba! Mrs. Zumba! Mrs. Zumba!* And a person came by and said, "Oh my God, it's Mother's Day. Are you doing this for a friend of yours, taking care of the kids?" And she goes, "No, no, these are my children." I remember the woman was just looking at her. With a deadpan look, Mom said to her, "Well, what do your children call *you?*" Joann and I, because we were the oldest, we got it, and we knew that Mom was just tired of seven kids saying "Mom!" 140 times apiece over the course of eighteen hours: she had had enough. For one day, she just wanted to be called by something else. I recognized at that moment that Mom really was her own person—despite the fact that we lived in an eight-hundred-square-foot home with one bathroom and with all the girls in one room and the boys in another room.

Then after twenty-five years of raising us pretty much on her own, her life changed. I was in my early twenties when I learned about it, and Joe, the youngest, was sixteen. How did you find out?

Jenevieve: Mom came to my apartment. I was seventeen years old and living on my own already. She called up and said, "I'd like to come over; I need to tell you something." I actually thought that maybe she was telling me she was getting married. She asked that we spend time alone, so my boyfriend left and I went out to Sizzler's with her. She proceeded to tell me that she'd had a calling and that she'd been feeling it for about two years, that she'd been accepted into this order, and that she was going to become a Catholic nun.

Annette: I think Mom was very, very troubled when she knew she was going to be leaving the family and not be the mother anymore.

Jenevieve: Oh, I absolutely think that—because although she felt all the love and all the connection to the church, she also felt the trouble and the grief of leaving her seven children.

The roughest part for me about Mom going into the convent was that suddenly I didn't have parents. That was absolutely frightening; I felt almost orphaned by the situation. I felt like, *What do I do for holidays?* At the time, I was applying to college. Everybody else went home to their parents in the summers. What was I going to do? Go stay in the convent? It sounds silly, but I couldn't do that.

My best friend at the time was a gal named Leslie. She was Catholic, and I remember Leslie telling me that Mom was just getting the best of both worlds: she got to get pregnant, be married and have a husband, and then go be a nun. It was a very interesting situation, because I really did see Mom's calling; I really saw the grace in it, the love and the commitment and everything else. But at the same time I was feeling completely abandoned.

There were a number of nuns who were not happy when Mom went in the convent. Just as my friend Leslie had expressed some issues about her getting the best of both worlds, some of the older nuns felt that too. It was exceedingly rare to get to become a Catholic nun after being married, having children, and being divorced. They gave her the papal dispensations—the pope actually signed a paper.

I called the convent almost every day to talk to her. When I'd call and I'd ask, "Can I talk to my mom?" the sisters would not be too happy about that.

Annette: Someone found Mom collapsed on the ground at the convent—she'd had an allergic reaction to a medicine—and they rushed her to the hospital in Santa Monica. The only reason we found out about it was that our brother Tony called up Mom, and a nun answered. She said, "Oh, I'm sorry. Your mom's not here." "Well, where is she?" "Well, she'll be in in a couple days." "Well, where *is* she?" "Well, there was an incident and she's in the hospital in the ICU."

Tony called me. I went to the ICU desk at the hospital, and I said, "I'm here to see my mother, Sister Jane Kelly." They said, "I'm sorry, nuns don't have children." I stood there, and I thought I was going to be one of these screaming women. Instead I said, "My mom has bigger goals in life than just to be Sister Jane Kelly—she's also a mom of seven kids. *Where is she?*" It seemed I was very disrespectful, but I was so determined to see her. When I saw her across the room, her head was the size of a basketball. She turned around, and she goes, "Oh, dear, you didn't have to come. I could fare on my own." I thought, *But why should you have to?* That was her grace.

I remember growing up as a Catholic girl and going to Catholic boarding school, I was never disrespectful to the sisters, but this was my mother. So I went to the head of the sisters and said, "The truth of the matter is, whether you like it or not, Sister Jane is the mother of seven children, and she is not going to die without one of us being there." Mom said that the relationship between her and the nuns changed after that night. It became apparent to them that they were being a bit selfish about her situation.

Jenevieve: I think all seven of us really adore Mom, and we all supported Mom going to the convent. The day she took her vows all seven of us were there, and it was like watching a wedding: it was this stunning thing. I think we all really believed that she should have the right to make that choice. We became disconnected to her so she could become connected to them.

Recorded in Sacramento, California, on April 26, 2008.

JENEVIEVE ZUMBA (*left*) AND
ANNETTE ZUMBA (*right*)

DOT CAMPI, 79

talks with her daughter,

KIM CAMPI, 51

Dot Campi: I always hoped for three or four children and a good life. It was never my thought that I would get married and be divorced in ten years—people didn't get divorced back then. So I was really very offended that my first husband wanted a divorce. I thought I was this great person—who is he to tell me he didn't want me? However, that's what happened. And I said, "I'm never gonna get married again." I was thirty-two.

I met Ronnie through a friend of mine. He was widowed—his first wife died at a very young age. We got talking, and he said he was looking for a mother for his five kids. So I said, "Well don't look at me!" You know what happened there.

People used to say to me, "You're marrying this guy with five kids—are you nuts?" I'd say, "Well, I love him, and I'll learn to love the kids." In the end, I used to tell Ronnie quite often, "You know, you're lucky you had these kids, because I never would've stayed here without them!"

Ronnie had five children: Pat was eighteen; Georgia was sixteen; Bobbie was thirteen; you, Kimmy, were around four, and David was two. My daughter Mona was ten, and then we had three together. Those are the three families that we blended together and blended very well, I think.

Kim Campi: What were your fears going into it?

Dot: At that particular time it was, *How am I gonna be a mother to all these kids?* One of the biggest fears was that your mom was dead. You could've put her on a pedestal, and she could've been this saint of saints. Here I am, this lowly person, coming into this family—how could I measure up? Not so much as a wife but as a mother. That was a really big concern.

I was tough. And I was as strict with the Campi kids as I was with the Romano kid or the Campi kids that Ronnie and I had together. I was an equal opportunity mother for strictness. And most of it was because Daddy worked so much of the time that the disciplining was left up to me. But never once, in all the time, did Daddy ever say, "Don't talk to my child like that!"—never never never never never. He always backed me up, and he told other people the same thing. He said, "Anything as far as discipline and behavior, that's Dot's job." And that's how we did it.

At one point I remember getting into a discussion with your older sister, Bobbie, and I said to her, "If you don't want me here, I'll leave!" She ran off and slammed the door, and I said, "Nobody slams doors in this house! You come down and we'll talk it over." She stayed upstairs for a little while. Then she came back down and she said, "I don't want you to leave."

Kim: You had rules: no elbows at the table; fifteen-minute limits on phone calls—and the phone would go in the bread drawer at dinner. You were involved in our lives but not to the point where you controlled us. I had a friend in third grade who came over the house, and you didn't tell me not to play with her, you just said, "I'm not crazy about her." That always stuck with me—that you never said, "You can't do this or be with that person." But you let us know how you felt and we respected you so we would follow that.

You were always consistent. You didn't have one rule one day and another the next—and you were loving at the same time, there was never any doubt that you loved us.

Dot: I really loved and tried to understand each child. You can't give every kid the same thing. The two boys, David and Joe, couldn't be more different, but look what happens when they see each other—you see what they do? They embrace and kiss each other—and they're not ashamed to do that. They change their nephews' diapers. It was like, *This is what you do as a family member—it doesn't matter who you are.* And I think I would say that about all my children.

One of the things that I remember is you and David called me "Lady." It was, "Lady, Lady," and one of the cutest things you told me was, "You know, Lady, my mother had red shoes." You were three and a half. Do you remember that?

Kim: I do remember that. [*laughs*]

Dot: We were very careful about using the word "stepmother," because we're a very united family. And *half* really doesn't work for me, either. [*laughs*] Maybe that's why we blended so well, because we didn't say, *Well, that's your mom and that's your dad.* It was: *This is my brother. This is my sister. This is my mother. This is my father.* Maybe that sounds a little like bragging, but I really believe that's why.

You know, I do regret that my first marriage didn't work. I wish that I could've made that marriage a success. But then I think, *Gee, all I would have is Mona and that little family—and look what I have now!*

Just recently, someone said to me that one thing they love is coming into my house and looking at those nine pictures over the piano. They would say, "Now, wait a minute, which one is yours? Which ones are Ronnie's and which ones are the ones you had together?" They wouldn't know the difference. Somebody said, "All I remember is nine pictures on the wall." I think that that's the secret of what made us a good family. And that would be, I think, my greatest success. My family. All of you.

Recorded in New York, New York, on August 19, 2009.

LOURDES VILLANUEVA, 49

speaks with her son,

ROGER VILLANUEVA JR., 30

Lourdes Villanueva: I always felt that I was blessed because I was born right at the border. We lived on the Mexico
side of the river, and for years my dad went to Texas to work
during the week, and Friday he would come home. So that's
how it went for several years, until we had a hurricane that
destroyed everything. At the time, he was working in Mississippi, and it was not very easy for him to get back to us. He
said, "No more of this. We will be together as a family through
thick and thin, and we're just going to have to make it work."
This, of course, began our journey, first into Texas and then
all over the country, picking crops.

When we started traveling, we always saw it as an adven-
ture. I never felt we were poor or *Oh, poor me*. It was like, *We're
going to go to a different place. We're going to meet new people and
do a different type of work*. That's something that I have to thank

my parents for. They always made us feel good about what we were doing—it was something that needed to be done, and we just happened to be the ones to do it.

Neither one of my parents had an education. They were very hardworking people. My dad was always like, "You don't really need to go to school. You need to work—if you're a hard worker, then that's all you need." My mother was the one that said, "No. You need to go to school!" Everywhere we went, even if we were going to be there for four weeks or six weeks picking the crops, she would make sure that they enrolled us in school.

I started to go to school in Texas. The whole town were Mexicans, but Spanish was not allowed in the schools. They used to have little playground patrols, which were supposed to turn you in if you were speaking Spanish. I didn't know English, but I was still going to talk, so I was always in trouble. My mother had to come get me because they let her know that I was being bad, speaking Spanish. Finally one day my poor mom said, "Please, don't talk any more—I can't keep picking you up!"

The ninth grade was when you started working for credits to graduate, and we never stayed in one place long enough. So after two years of trying to compile some credits, I thought, *I'm going to be in the ninth grade forever!* You know, I was sixteen, so why even bother? So I dropped out of the ninth grade, and I got married at eighteen and had you.

You pretty much grew up in the back of the pickup truck. On my breaks, I'd come and change your diaper and do whatever needed to be done so that I could continue working. There was you, and then Anna, and when Oscar came along, Barbara from the migrant workers' agency asked me, "What are you going to do?" "What do you mean what am I going to do? I'm a grown woman and I'm raising my children." "Well, you should go back to school." I remember thinking, *If you only knew—we work all day, and we work all night, and we move everywhere, so what do you mean "go to school"?* But it was that little seed—*Maybe there's something there.*

Your father and I agreed that we wanted our kids to finish school and go to college. That meant we had to hurry up and save some money so that you could go to school in one place. So when you started kindergarten, we thought we would stop moving. Of course, it didn't work out like that—we had a big freeze and there was no work, so we still had to travel. But we had that goal to stop moving so that you guys could go to school.

I knew that we didn't have wealth to leave you guys. So I always thought that my responsibility was to leave you a legacy of honesty, integrity, and education—and that was why I shoved it down your throat from day one, to all three of you. I would always say, "You need to do what I didn't do, which is finish your education."

Roger Villanueva: You always said that you were going

119

to lead by example and that you weren't just going to tell us what to do. I remember when you went back and got your GED. You had three kids in the back of the truck and you were in the fields, but during break times you had your books out and you would be studying instead of having lunch. Dad was the one to take care of us and cook for us when you were out four or five hours a night getting your GED.

I remember we hated beans and eggs—that's what we ate every night because that's all Dad knew how to cook. He's like, "Well, be happy that you at least have beans and eggs to eat, because there's a lot of people that don't even have that." He used to make us eat everything because he wanted us to appreciate everything that we had. I can remember us stuffing the food under the refrigerator, thinking that you all wouldn't know, and then we would act like our plates were done.

After that, I remember you said, "I'm going to go to community college." I remember you taking a class here and there, and then sometimes work got to the point where you had to drop courses. But the next semester you picked them up again, and I remember times where you had to take the same class over and over again because of something or another. Raising three kids, trying to hold down the house front and your job—you were always on the go, and for you to put school on your plate was just really hard. Just like you're proud of us, I was just *so* proud that day that you graduated. It took you a little bit longer—

Lourdes: I had to hurry up and graduate before you guys did, because I knew you guys were coming right behind me!

Roger: Yeah, well, I took my detours, but I finally did it. I'm proud, because, like you said, that's something that nobody can take away from me.

Lourdes: I think one thing that I owe to my mother is that she felt that you always need to look at the positive side of things and never grow bitter, because sometimes it is easy for people to get discouraged and bitter about things that don't go right or that you feel are unfair. So I tried to push on you guys that you need to prove yourselves. Don't just wait for that door to open—you need to open the door and prove that you can do it and do it better. I know that I was a little hard on you guys—

Roger: I don't think anybody else loved us enough to give us that tough love. Only the people that really love you look out for you, and that's why you pushed us. To this day I still think that had it not been for you pushing me to go to college, to get my education, I don't think I would have made it. I can honestly tell you that.

From the bottom of my heart, I'm glad you did everything that you did. If I was to have the option to choose another mother, I would never choose anybody else but you. When I look for my partner, I always say, *If my wife can be half the woman that my mother is, I will be okay*. I know I've never told you that, but that's the way I feel.

Recorded in Tampa, Florida, on December 3, 2008.

MARTHA WELCH MENDEZ, 48

talks to her friend,

CATHY NICKELS, 44

about her mother, Ann Hils Welch.

Martha Welch Mendez: I was born here in Indianapolis, and my father's family has been here over a hundred years. I have six sisters and six brothers, and the age span is fifteen and a half years. I'm number nine, one of the little kids. My dad had a heart attack when she was pregnant with the last one—my youngest brother never got to meet my dad—so we had that real all-for-one, we're-all-in-this-together kind of thing. But we were pretty lucky, because my mom was very organized, very on time. She had a schedule: dinner was at 6:00 P.M., rain, shine, snow, no electricity, whatever—you just stuck to the routine. My cousin used to say that his house was the free world and our house was a communist country, because it was just so routine and regimented.

We had chores. We were responsible for setting the table and cleaning up. My day was Saturday, so I did the Saturday lunch dishes and the Saturday night dishes, and I set the table and helped with dinner. We helped with the laundry, folding the clothes, putting the clothes away, keeping the yard up—we all had chores. Cleaning the bathrooms was my least favorite, as you can imagine with all those people.

My mom went back to work as a nurse when I was in sixth or seventh grade. About twenty-five years later, she was still working part-time, but things weren't adding up. She wasn't acting like herself, so we insisted she go to the doctor. And she kind of dragged her feet. Finally she did go, and they did all kinds of tests, and they ruled everything else out and came with the diagnosis of Alzheimer's, which she didn't want to believe. She kept saying, "I just hope I don't have that." But she had a whole file at home of articles and clippings she had cut out about Alzheimer's. She knew.

I think we caught it so early because she was always so on top of everything, and she kept saying things that just didn't make sense. It was very hard to see that. My sister came to visit with my two nephews and my niece. My nephew got up early, and my mom fed him breakfast. About half an hour later she told him it was time to eat breakfast again. She fed the poor kid four breakfasts that morning—he was too polite to say anything.

We were fortunate in finding it out early, so we could enjoy her. She hasn't known us for a long time, though she seems to know that you're there to see her or that you're connected to her somehow. I don't know how to explain that feeling—

you'll be in the dining room and there will be forty-some people there, but she seems to understand that you're there for her. When my daughter was a baby, I had her sitting in my mom's lap. My mom had not said my name in several years, not seemed to know who I was, and she leaned down and she kissed my daughter on the top of her head and said, "Martha's baby." Which just about floored me.

One day I went to visit her, and she thought she worked there; she was helping this woman to the bathroom. The woman was asking my mom about how many children she had. Well, it was obvious my mom did not remember, so I said, "Mom, do you remember how many boys you had?" And she said, "No." I said, "Do you remember how many girls?" And she said "No." Then she says, "Well, smarty pants, how many

kids do I have?" And so I said, "Mom, you have thirteen children." And she said, "What? Was I crazy??" It was so funny because she had absolutely no idea that that was her life, but she had managed it exceptionally well.

Recorded in Indianapolis, Indiana, on September 22, 2007.

CATHY NICKELS (*left*) AND
MARTHA WELCH MENDEZ (*right*)

SHARON CAPRA, 54

Sharon Capra: My husband went into the air force in 1976, and soon after I got pregnant with my firstborn son, Tony. Eleven other siblings came after that, and I'll say their names right now: Jason, James, Michael, Rachel, Sarah, Joseph, Jacob, Danielle, Joanna, Julia, and Emily.

My husband was a missile launch officer and he also did OSI [Office of Special Investigations], and so he was gone a lot, and many times Tony was the oldest in the home. He liked to be the man of the house. He would take the dog for a walk when he was four—I don't know if the dog walked him or he walked the dog. And he was always wanting to do the big guy stuff—you know, take the trash out—all you saw was the trash can, you didn't see the kid. [*laughs*] When I was really busy with the children and Tony was in the car with me, many times I'd pull up to the front of a supermarket or a post office and he would run in there and do all the errands. He thought that it was fun to be a "guy," you know, to be a man. He really wanted to be like his dad.

When he was a young child, he would wear his father's BDUs [battle dress uniforms] and walk around the house and say he was a soldier. That seemed like his career choice from very young on. He would tell me, "Mom, buy me some military books." He seemed fascinated with war strategy, which seemed boring to me. I said, "Look, can't I buy you a different book?" and he'd say, "No, it really fascinates me!" So I would. When everything would get crazy in the house, he'd retreat to his bedroom, close the door, and read those books.

When I would get the children to bed, sometimes he and I would sit up and watch movies and eat popcorn. One time I told him, "You know, I just loved you so much, I wanted to have more children because you were just so great." He said, "Well, Mom, logically, I think that you should've had just me. If you really liked me so much, you didn't need anybody else!"

He was very smart and very quick to grasp ideas, but he wanted to always think of ways that he could improve them. I would show him a math problem, and I would say, "This is the formula." And he'd say, "I bet I could do it in a different way." So he would try to figure out another way to get around it. At the time it was very frustrating. I thought, *Can't you just do it the way I'm telling you to do it?* But he would try to figure out a different way. He'd say, "Mom, you said that it's not right to do something, but why?" One time, he listened to the radio and heard about homosexuals wanting to be parents, and he said, "You know, I don't understand why they can't be just as good parents as a heterosexual couple." He would challenge me to think outside the box.

He opened my eyes to the fact that children are not just little mes—they're their own people, and they have their own opinions. We raised our children to be Christians, but as the years went on I realized that even though I value something, my children have to decide what their values are and how they're going to define themselves. You can guide and encourage, but eventually they have to make those choices. There were times when I didn't like it, but that's what life is about.

When Tony graduated from high school, he met Angie. I was in labor with my eleventh child, and he came running into my labor room and said, "Mom! Mom, I met the most beautiful woman in the world!" and I said, "Tony, not right now, I'm in labor!" He said, "No, I've got to tell you about her! She's just gorgeous!" I was in *labor*—I thought, *Man, he's really fallen for this woman.*

Eight months later he married her. He tried to get into the air force because the baby was coming and he needed a job. They said, "You had asthma as a boy, so we can't let you in"—there was this one little episode where he had a respiratory syndrome. But he kept calling back, and the last time he called they said, "You've pestered us enough, and you only had one episode of this when you were two years old, so we're going to go ahead and let you come in." He called me up and said, "Mom, I got into the military!" He was really excited.

When I became a grandma, Tony called me on the phone, and he goes, "Mom! Mom, listen!" I heard crying, and he goes, "Mom, he's just so awesome! Mom, he's so healthy, and his little eyes are just so bright!" He just wouldn't let him go. He stayed there all day and just held him. He was really happy to be a father.

Tony decided on EOD, which is explosive ordnance disposal. I was upset, and so was his wife. We wanted him to be safe, to choose a safe career path: *How about the library?* [*laughs*] But there was always something in him that was more daring. So when he told us his choice, I thought, *Yeah, that's what he would do*. I still didn't want him to do it, but he wasn't going to change his mind.

So that's what he did, and he really, thoroughly loved it. He did two missions to Afghanistan and two to Iraq. He didn't like being away from his family, of course—that was his number one priority. By then he had five children, and he loved being with them, but he provided for his family really well and he thought that he was doing what he was supposed to do.

When he had his own family, our relationship changed— I had to let him go. It was hard, but I let him be who he was, and I was just extremely proud of him. I think that's probably the miracle of parenting: over time, you think—you *know*—it's just a miracle to see who they become as people.

I didn't talk to Tony that often when he was in Iraq. A lot of my information would come from his brothers. He would diligently call them—but he didn't want to worry me. If I wanted to hear anything, I had to hear it from someone else—I'd overhear his brothers talking, but they wouldn't tell me very much either. I think they were all just trying to protect Mom.

He had volunteered to go to Iraq the second time—his fourth mission—and it was there that he was hit by an IED. We just didn't expect it. He had had some close calls while he was over there, but we just assumed that he would make it through again and he was going to come home soon. There was just no doubt in our minds. . . .

Angie lived about an hour away, and there were two teams coming to both homes at the same time to tell us. When we were told, I had my hands over my ears and I fell to the ground screaming, "*No!*" And his father just tried to hold it together and said, "Was there anybody else hurt?" and "Where's my son now?"

We drove over to Angie's and all their kids were playing outside. Angie and I started hugging and crying, and my husband goes, "You know, we don't need to cry, because Tony did something very brave and we're proud of him." And then he said, "And that was my son. . . ." And he just couldn't talk—he started to cry. I had never seen my husband cry before . . . and I saw how much his son meant to him.

My son lived. In his thirty-one years, he lived. Tony wanted to be in the military. He knew the dangers. He chose it. When I'm with my grandchildren, I'll gather them around and I'll talk to them about their father, and they're very excited to listen. They want to know who their dad was. I want them to remember him with a smile. He was a character. But he was also brave, and I want them to be brave, too—to be courageous and to stand for what they think is right. People look back and remember you for the things you did for others, for the courage to live your life the way you thought you should, and for showing people that you love them. Life is more than just about you—and I think my son showed that through his life and through his death.

Recorded in Arlington, Virginia, on July 11, 2009.

ENDURING
LOVE

KRISTI HAGER, 59

tells her friend,

CHERIE NEWMAN, 52

about her mom, Norine Hager.

Kristi Hager: I've been thinking about my mom a lot. In a couple of days, I'm going to be giving her eulogy, and I have an awful lot of stories to tell that I won't be able to tell in ten minutes. She was spunky. She liked to get us out of the house in the summertime. She would say things like "Get out and shake the stink off!" She couldn't stand us sitting around. Somebody who wrote me a condolence note said, "Your mom was rock solid," and that's a quality that really rings true to me. Because she was from the Midwest, she had a real solid, no-nonsense attitude towards life. I'm going to miss that.

I remember moments when my mother and I shared completely blissful laughing fits. The kind where something gets you going, and you start laughing—and you know you're laughing just because you're laughing. Then you don't know *why* you're laughing, so you're laughing at the fact that you don't know why you're laughing. . . .

One of the things that triggered one of those fits was when I was helping her study for her lifesaving exam so she could be a lifeguard at our swimming pond. I was about nine years old. I would read her the questions, and she had the answers memorized. She had it down. So I asked her the question: "What do you do when you're swimming in a pond and the weeds below start to pull you under?" And she just answered, "Extricate yourself with slow, undulating motions." The words came out of her mouth and we both looked at each other and burst into this laughing fit—sides *aching*! I didn't even know what it meant; I just knew that it was the funniest thing I had ever heard. She was laughing so hard until we didn't even know why we were laughing anymore.

I got into that state with my mother probably two or three times in my life, and that was when we weren't mother and daughter anymore. Those roles just kind of fell by the wayside, and at those moments we were just two people laughing. It's a transcendent moment, and I treasure it. I kind of forgot about those words for years and years and years, but that moment of laughter I never forgot.

I feel a certain longing. It's a very animal type of longing. My enduring image is her sitting with the other mothers in the neighborhood while she watched us swimming in the pond. I just have this image of her sitting with her knees in front of her and her arms resting on her knees and her back was so tan. Right now I just think of that warm back, and I just want to put my cheek next to it. It's just visceral. Her presence there on the shore was so reassuring.

Recorded in Missoula, Montana, on August 4, 2005.

EILEEN COHEN, 56

talks to her husband,

JAMIE ROY, 52

about her mother, Helen Cohen.

Eileen Cohen: My mom worked three jobs, so all the household tasks happened on the weekend. My brothers and I would be sleeping, and she would be in the supermarket—early, early, early. She'd drag all the groceries up the steps. We were kinda rousing out of the bed, and we would try to help her. But being a traditional Jewish mother, she wasn't interested. She would say, "The horse is here"—she being the horse. "The horse can work from morning till night. My big lump"—that was Jeffrey—"my little lump"—that was Mark—"and my middle lump"—that was me. "Go back to bed, my three little lumps, because the horse is here!" I guess it was typical Jewish guilt. And that went on for years.

It was impossible not to fall in love with her. It was *impossible*. Children fell in love with her; some kids would go over to her and say, "Could you take me home and be my grandma?" They just absolutely loved her.

Jamie Roy: She reminds me a lot of you—and I fell in love with you. The story that's always amazed me is the time you were in the Caribbean and you got dragged out to sea.

Eileen: I had a job with a pacemaker company, and one of the sales reps asked me if I wanted to go on vacation. He said, "We're gonna get a sailboat, a big one, and we're gonna sail in the Caribbean." And I said, "Count me in! Absolutely." But the problem was, I didn't know how to swim.

About a week before the vacation, I said to a lifeguard, "I'm going on vacation in the Caribbean. I don't know how to swim—can you teach me?" He looked at me and said, "There's no way I can do this in a week—how about if I just teach you how to tread water?" I said, "Fine, teach me how to do that." So he did.

We were on this great boat, sailing, and I decided to jump in the water. I felt very confident because I had flippers on and it was salt water, so I was very buoyant. I thought I would go exploring. So I did—and I was sucked out into the ocean. I yelled, but there was huge wind, and they couldn't hear me. I yelled, "Help me! Help me! Help me!" I was in the ocean by myself, and the boat where I had originally jumped in was a distant, distant vision.

I think it was the one time in my life that I didn't analyze or think. I was just on automatic pilot. And my mother was with me the entire time. I heard her from the moment I realized that I couldn't get back. Every time I started panicking, I heard her say to me, "You're my special girl. Don't worry, you can do this. You've done things that you thought were hard before. Remember when you didn't know how to skip, and I taught you how to skip? You were so upset. Hang in there!"

One of my vacationmates called my mother and father to say that I'm missing at sea, presumed dead, because the harbormaster said, "If she doesn't know how to swim, it's impossible she could last out there." So my father answered, and he said, "I don't know what you're talking about—you took her away alive; you better bring her back exactly like that! I'm not interested in anything else that you have to say."

When I was in the ocean, I saw in the distance a little piece of land. I've seen people swim; I knew you had to use your arms and kick your legs. So I kind of did that until I was finally able to get to that piece of land. It was deserted, but the next day, I had a plan: to sit on one of the rocks that jutted out into the ocean, take the ribbon out of my hair, put it on a stick, and sit and wait there till a boat came by, and try to get their attention. Which is exactly what happened.

When I was brought back to my friends, I called my mom and my dad from the harbor to tell them that I was okay, and my mother said, "Listen, I realize you're twenty-eight years old, but this vacation's over as far as I'm concerned. I'm sending your brother down to get you." She sent Mark down, and when I met him at the airport, he said, "Mom stayed up the whole night. She was talking to you. She paced back and forth

saying, 'You're my special girl. You can do this. You're strong.'"
Exactly what I heard while treading water.

I feel it was really an honor and a privilege to be her child, I really do. In her eyes, there were only three children in the entire world: there were the three of us, and then everyone else was underneath. And it wasn't that she didn't really love everybody else, because she'd stop and look at every child and talk to every mother. But *her* children—no one could compare.

She made you feel loved, adored, cherished, and *safe*.

Recorded in Springfield, Massachusetts, on September 6, 2008.

ROBERT MADDEN, 44

talks to his friend,

TOM KURTHY, 44

about his mother, Betty Jane Madden.

Robert Madden: I grew up in south central Mississippi. My mom and dad were both country people, and the gifts that they gave me are astounding to me today. I grew up in a country environment: I laugh about not wearing shoes until I went to school—it was pretty true. We would go visit my grandmother and drive a mile down a country road, through the cattle guard, and down behind cornfields to get to her house. I thought everyone grew up like we did.

I woke up every morning of my life, from the time I started school until I finished high school, to my mother saying, "Robert Lynn, Robert Lynn, wake up, honey! Breakfast is on the table!" She'd get up every morning, she'd make breakfast, and when I'd come home from school in the afternoon, there was always something fresh baked. Then I'd do my homework, and she'd send us out to play. Then at six or six-thirty, dinner was on the table, from scratch. I took all that for granted growing up. I went to pick up a friend to take him to school one morning—his mother was still in bed, and there were vodka bottles all over his dining room table, and she was screaming, "Get your own breakfast!" And I was like, "Is this normal?" And he's like, "Oh yeah, totally normal for me."

My mom was called the Bicycle Lady when I was a kid because she rode eighteen miles on her bike every day. It didn't matter if it was raining or whatever, she would put on her poncho, and she'd take off on her bike. I just loved being with her. She was an amazing woman. *Stubborn*. I got a double dose of that.

My mother was Catholic and my father was Southern Baptist, and in the 1950s it was unheard of that they would get married. My dad was a southern gentleman to his core, a country southern gentleman. And he loved his kids and his family more than anything—but he loved my mother most. That's one of the things that for me is so beautiful still— the love that they shared. He loved Hank Williams and Patsy Cline, and I can still see him and my mom dancing in the living room when they didn't think anybody was watching. My mom passed away from cancer in October of 2006, and six months later my father died of a broken heart—he even told his doctor that's what was wrong with him. The power of their love was amazing. They were a sassy, spicy, beautiful, exciting, vibrant couple. Their life together was whole and beautiful.

I'd come out to my parents when I was ten: I told them that I was going to marry a man when I grew up. But that was a kind of childhood question—I was constantly asking questions of the nature of things, and Mother would say, "Ask the priest, honey—I don't know. I don't know who God's mother is. I don't know where the edge of the universe is. . . . I don't know."

My mother had always told me, "We can handle anything as a family as long as you tell us first. I don't want to hear about it through the grapevine." So when I decided to start living openly gay, I told them. My father told me, "I've known since you were a little boy. It doesn't matter to me if you spend your life with a man or with a woman, as long as you make it something you can hold your head up about." I was astounded. It was just such open, beautiful acceptance. Every year after that he would just tell me how proud he was of me and the way that I lived my life.

My mother took some time, because she thought it was her fault—she felt guilty about it. My grandmother's passing is what really stimulated her to call me, because my grandma had said, "You're missing out on a beautiful relationship with Robert Lynn because you can't accept this about him. He's Robert Lynn. He's still the same person you raised and that we all grew up with." My grandmother loved me very much, and she and my mom and I were sort of this triangle of strength in the family. So my mother came around.

I remember once I went home to visit my mom and dad. My mom and I used to have these really incredible conversations after everyone else went to bed. This particular night she asked me if I would stay up with her, and then she just started asking me all these questions: "What was sex like between two men?" All that kind of stuff. She said, "If you're embarrassed then you don't need to answer." And I said, "I'm not embarrassed. I'm just shocked you would ask me." And she was like, "I want to know. I've been out of your life too long, and I want to know." So I explained to her, and she sat there with a straight face. Afterwards she just went, "Hmm, curious."

The last ten years, I made a point to spend as much time with her as I could. A lot of times I would go when I knew none of my siblings would be there, so I could be alone with my parents. I wouldn't trade those times for anything in the world. I could go there and just get all that sustenance and all that joy and love and acceptance.

When my mother was passing, she put her hand on my face and she said, "You are so precious. I love you." I said, "I love you too, Mom." And she goes, "No, I mean *unconditionally*." It was the greatest gift . . . it was just the greatest gift she could have given me.

I lost both my parents this past year, six months apart. I know I'll get through it because you're with me, but some days I just feel like I can't breathe, you know? But I do feel them all around me.

When my father was passing he used to say that he could see my mother in the room, that she was there. "Don't you see her?" he'd say. "Isn't she beautiful?"

Recorded in Santa Monica, California, on November 9, 2007.

TOM KURTHY (*left*) AND
ROBERT MADDEN (*right*)

HILORY BOUCHER, 61

talks to her son,

DAVE MILLS, 42

Hilory Boucher: Skip and I were classmates at Boston University. He was cute, and everybody liked him. We just sort of got together and double-dated with this girl in my dorm and a friend of his. His friend had a car, so we sat in the backseat, and after we'd go bowling and get ice cream, we'd park the car and neck.

We went to babysit for his sister's child in their apartment. We planned this whole thing—this was going to be *it*. I don't think he had any more experience than I did. It was not very romantic, and we were both embarrassed. Finally, the deed was accomplished, and we talked about, "Oh, could I get pregnant?" In your mind, you just think, *No, not me. God's going to take care of me—I'm going to get away with this.*

We had broken for summer vacation, and I went home with my family in Connecticut. I told my mother, "I didn't get my friend." She said, "Well you certainly couldn't be pregnant, could you?" I said, "No, no! Not me, no!" Totally in denial, until finally she decided I should see the doctor. Our family doctor had delivered my brothers and sisters, had set broken bones, pierced my *ears* for heaven sakes—everything—so this is the man who examined me, the first time I'd ever been examined that way, and he said to me, "You're pregnant. Would you like me to tell your mother, or do you want to tell your mother?" I said to him, "I can't tell my mother." Fortunately, he did. My mother was holding back tears, just *mortified*. She said nothing to me until we were in the car, and then she said, "I'm going to have to let your father know this." So that was the day of reckoning.

My father was a man who expected a certain respect from us, I think even more than love. We were raised Roman Catholic. We attended Mass every Sunday and went to religious instruction. In high school I was never one of the kids who went out drinking—I just always wanted to be good. Well, now I'd done something that was *totally* out of the realm of what was expected of me.

My mother and father did not want their friends to know I was pregnant, and I've only found out recently how few of them did know. One of my mother's best friends had no idea. I think what they really find incredible is that my mother didn't confide in them. I think it was just a tremendous disappointment to my parents, and they didn't want to tell people that I'd messed up or maybe that they'd messed up.

My parents had met Skip, and they liked him. I thought,

Well, I'm going to have to get married. It didn't happen. His parents did not know about our relationship, and they would not have liked him going out with a girl who wasn't Jewish. So his brother-in-law got me a place in the Florence Crittenton Home for unwed mothers in a suburb of Boston.

It was a pleasant place to be. We ate together in a dining room; we all took turns at different tasks in the kitchen and in cleaning. It was like an initiation—you'd meet other people in the same situation as you, get to know them, and find out how many people are just like you. We knitted baby clothes and read baby magazines. I made a bunny, a pink bunny, which—

Dave Mills: I still have to this day.

Hilory: And you didn't know until recently that I had made it for you—the fact that you kept it all this time without that knowledge!

I went into labor the day before or the day after you were due. I remember one girl who delivered about the same time I did—she did not want to see her baby. She said, "I'm glad it's out of me! I want to be away from here and go on with my life!" She was angry with herself, she was angry with everybody, and she was angry with the baby. In my case, I said, "I want to feed my baby." So they would bring you in during the day. At night, they said, "You're going to need your sleep," but during the day, every two hours, they'd bring you to me. And I *savored* it. I was there for a couple of weeks—they used to keep you in the hospital for a while.

My social worker was very upset. "You said you didn't want to see the baby beforehand. What's changed?" I said, "I delivered him, and now I want to see him. I've changed my mind." I actually thought, "I'm going to keep him somehow— I just can't imagine giving a child away."

Dave: You told me that you left the hospital with me, which is not normally done.

Hilory: My mother came up to Massachusetts, picked us up, and drove us back to Connecticut. You were handed off to a social worker at a stop on the Merritt Parkway, with your pink bunny and your layette. My mother was split and torn. If it wasn't for my father, you would probably have been with us, but my dad was the one who didn't even want to see your picture. I know it was difficult for him, but this was the decision he had made.

I thought of you every birthday and more often than that. It's funny, because I used to think, *I wonder if he's wondering today about the person that didn't want him.* I always worried, *I hope he doesn't think that I didn't love him.* I was hoping you would look for me. I was hoping, but I also thought if a person grows up happy with a family, I don't know if he would look for someone who gave him away.

I made the decision when I turned sixty that I was going to do a search—I needed to know before I died what happened to this child.

Dave: When I was a child growing up in a family with siblings that were all adopted, the fact that I was adopted was explained to me as early as I could understand it. I thought everybody was adopted—I thought that when parents have kids, they go to a building and pick them up. I can still remember, I was probably six or seven years old, and my friend was telling me how his mom was going to have a baby. My response was, "You mean she's going to keep him?" I thought that everybody just ended up going to somebody else's family.

Hilory: Isn't that a great thing to think that you're there by someone's choice—someone wanted a child so much that there you are—*I want you, you're mine.*

Dave: At least consciously, I never felt rejection over it. The reason I made the first steps to look for you was mostly curiosity. It wasn't something I was preoccupied with or stayed awake at night losing sleep over, but I just had this curiosity.

I'd been living in Ontario almost half a year. This letter came in the mail that had been forwarded from my last address. It came originally from Northport, New York. Pardon the expression, but I thought to myself, *Who the hell do I know in New York?* Which was nobody. I opened that envelope and read the first few lines, and my chin hit my lap. I never had a moment in my life where I was so stunned, where I physically couldn't read beyond that. This might sound melodramatic, but it changed my life.

Hilory: I had written that letter so long ago and it had been returned twice. The lady at the agency hadn't been able to find you, so we thought, *Well, that's that.*

Then you left me a voice mail message, and I was like, *Oh my God, I have to sit down!* It was just amazing when I called you and you answered! It was just like, *Hello, where have you been all my life?* Like we just picked up where we left off.

Dave: If you could have said anything to me as a five-year-old child, what would you have said?

Hilory: I would have said, "I hope that you're very happy. I hope your dad is good to you, and I hope your mom is a lady you love very much. I hope she's making chocolate chip cookies for you and playing in the snow with you. I hope she bakes you a cake on your birthday, and you blow out candles and sing!" Because that's what I was hoping would happen for you. And in fact, I think that's how it was.

Recorded in New York, New York, on August 15, 2007.

MYRA DEAN, 61

talks to her boyfriend,

GARY JAMISON, 58

Myra Dean: My son was Richard Damon Stark. People used to ask him what he wanted to be when he grew up, and he used to tell people he wanted to be a marine biologist or a garbage man. He wanted to be ten. He didn't make it. He was nine years and four months old when he died.

He and I had moved to a little house in Kansas City after I separated from his dad. I bought it because when I was looking at apartments, Rich kept getting more and more upset. I said, "Rich, why are you so upset?" He just kept saying, "Momma, I don't want to move to an apartment, I don't want to move to an apartment." And I said, "Why?" Finally he said it was because his little friend told him his mom got a divorce and they moved to an apartment and she got mean. So I took every apartment off the list and I thought, *I will find a house I can afford to buy.*

I found this little house, and it was perfect. Three weeks to the day after we moved in was May 13, 1977 and I was going to go out with my girlfriend. Rich had a new friend named Steve, and they were riding bikes. When I went to get the babysitter, I went down the street and said, "Come on, we've got to go." And he didn't want to go; he just wanted to stay and ride bikes with Steve. I thought to myself, *I don't want to tie him to his momma's apron strings*. Steve's mom was standing there, and she said, "We're going to go ride bikes. Just leave him here with me." I didn't have far to go, and so I said, "Watch for cars." And I left. When I came back, I pulled up in front of the little house, and I saw this crowd of people at the end of the street and ambulance lights.

I got out of the car, and I knew the minute I opened the car door and put my feet on the ground that it was Rich. I guess some people don't believe that you can know that, but I knew. I got out of the car and I just started running, and when I got there, there were people all around him. They wouldn't let me up to him. They were working on him, and they just sat me down. I had an out-of-body experience: I went up in the air, and I looked down, and I could see me sitting on the ground. I could see them working on Rich. They put him in the back of the ambulance, and they put me in a police car and we followed the ambulance. I just started screaming. I can still remember the face on the policeman—I think it about killed him. I remember him turning to me and saying, "Ma'am, I've got kids, too." I kept saying, "Even if my family comes, don't leave me, don't leave me!" And he didn't—he stayed right there with me. My ex-husband came. They took us in a hallway, and they just said, "There was nothing we could do. He's gone." I can remember having my back to the wall, and I just slid down, leaning against that wall.

Later I found out that a guy had been hot-rodding through our neighborhood. The car went airborne and over a six-foot hedge, and it landed on Rich and Steve. The car flipped over. Steve was caught where the hood and the windshield made like a little tent, but the car landed on Rich. They had pulled the driver out, and he kept saying, "Oh my God, what have I done? What have I done?" Steve's mom was a nurse, and even with her own son lying there, she tried to give Rich CPR.

The ambulance driver came to me at the hospital, and he said, "Ma'am, I'm not supposed to tell you this—but he was dead at the scene." He'll never know what that meant to me, because one of the things that was the hardest for me was, *What if he was suffering and I wasn't there for him?*

Steve's mother said the last thing that he said to her was, "My momma told me to watch for cars." He wasn't even in the street—they'd gone up into the yard. Steve's mom walked in the garage to get her bike to take them riding, and Richie wanted to go to that yard and sit and watch the sunset. So it's a bittersweet thing that he died watching the sunset.

I always try to find ways to explain to people about the

pain: It's as if you've had an invisible amputation, you know? When you lose your child it's like somebody has just amputated a huge chunk of your heart. The difference is people can't see the amputation.

When Rich died, I thought I wouldn't live ten minutes. I was astonished when I'd lived ten days and mortified when I'd lived ten months, and not even grateful yet when I had lived ten years. I was mostly surprised; there was no one more astonished that I'd survived it than myself. God, in his mercy, does not give you all of the impact at one time. You're just so numb for so long, and then it starts to seep in. After a year or two people think you should be getting better, but that's really when the shock is wearing off and you start to feel again. And oh my God, it's *so bad*. But fortunately, I found other people who had been through it, and they said, "It won't be like this forever," and it hasn't been.

I needed to be with other people that knew what was happening to me. I'd meet with other bereaved parents, and we'd talk about how you'd be at the grocery store with your cart, you'd come around the corner, and somebody at the other end would look up and see you, and you could see it on their faces—it was like they had rockets on the carts—they would just go and hit the next aisle. People would avoid even passing you in the grocery store, because God forbid they should say, "How are you doing?" and upset you. Seriously, people think after you lose a child if they don't mention it maybe you won't think about it. It's just insane.

I miss Rich terribly and I wonder what he would be like. He was just a happy kid, and he died watching the sunset. I used to have such terrible guilt about that, because I always used to think if I hadn't taught him to see everything that was around him, then he would have just been off riding his bike like a normal kid. He wouldn't have gone down to watch the sunset, and if he hadn't been in that yard, he wouldn't have been killed. You always think you can protect your children and you can't—it's such a feeling of helplessness and powerlessness.

Today I'm in a far better place—as they say, a far, far better place. In the story of Job, Job lost everything, and he got everything back twofold. With me, I have two great stepchildren that I raised: Mike and Sara. I'm their mom. I didn't have them, but they're mine.

I'm blessed and I'm loved, and I know that I've made a difference. If I was buried, I'd want my tombstone to say, "She made a difference." That's really the only thing that matters in this world.

Recorded in Abilene, Texas, on March 21, 2008.

JACKIE MILLER, 73

speaks with her son,

SCOTT MILLER, 39

Jackie Miller: You are one of the finest human beings I know. I love being around you. I've seen you become such a bold, brave individual. That's something I always wanted for myself. And when I'm looking at my life now, I think, *Go for it, Jackie. Go for it!* So I guess you learn from your kids.

Someone told me just this week: "If you see Scott in the elevator, I don't care what kind of a day you're having, you feel happier." When I hear people say stuff like that, I'm thinking, *I hope I had a part to play in that.* But I don't know how much credit your father and I can really take. I'd like to say you're so perfect because of all my efforts. [*laughs*] But I realize that you're your own unique self that nobody can really take credit for.

Scott Miller: I always grew up knowing that I was adopted, but I've never really understood what went into it—I guess probably because we never talked much about it. So when did you and Dad decide to adopt?

Jackie: We always knew from the time we first married—we're very methodical people. Our plan was: we're gonna get married, and two years later we're gonna have a child, and then we're going to adopt a child. Well, the two years go by, and we didn't have a biological child. *Okay, let's do the adoption thing.* And that's what we did.

For all the wonderful things I said about you before, you were truly a handful. I mean, you took all that we had. We had no time for anything else or anybody else—we really didn't. No energy. So we couldn't even consider, could not even *consider* a biological child after that. You were it, and we knew it.

Now, this is something you really don't know, and I don't know how you're gonna react to this. When I was seventeen years old, I got pregnant. The light of my life is my father, but he gave me twenty-four hours to leave town. I did have a son, at seventeen, but you don't have many resources, and I was not able to keep this child. I gave this little baby up for adoption, and I said, *I don't know how to make this right, but I will adopt a child when I'm able to take care of a child.* And that's what I did.

I always was going to tell you at some point—I just didn't know when. I know children tend to put their parents on pedestals, but I think I handled the situation as best I could. I wish it had never happened, but it did. . . .

Scott: . . . Wow.

Jackie: I know, I know. The thing is that there's not much we haven't talked about over the years. We love our talky sessions. So many times it would seem, *Gosh, is this the time to tell him?* But I'm seventy-three now. I don't know anybody else who's going to tell you, and I think you should know. It just seems like such a big secret, and I don't like having that out there.

Scott: Thank you for telling me. I just wasn't ready for that. [*laughs*] I just didn't know. And I love you for telling me. I can't believe that you've walked around for so many years with that—it had to be hard for you.

Jackie: The hardest part for me was that you bring a life into the world, and you really don't know anything about what happened. But I always thought about him.

Scott: Wow . . . Speaking of secrets, I remember when I came out to you. We met for dinner in Harlem. I remember still not really knowing how you were going to react and being scared, thinking, *Okay, here we go!* I remember saying to you, "Hey, Mom, I want to talk to you about something." And you took your glasses off, and you put them on the table. You buckled your fingers and looked at me—almost through me. I remember thinking, *Oh my God, this is awful!* I stumbled just telling you I was gay. And you looked away. Then the first thing out of your mouth was "I love you, and I'm your mother." I just remember everything kind of melting away.

Jackie: By that time, I knew—it wasn't even a question in my mind. Just as you were this wonderful little kid with all the curiosity, you were gay—that was as much a part of you as any of the other things. It's just you. It was certainly never a choice you had.

Your gayness has brought such dimension to my life. I'm just on the fringes of it, but I see such a community of care and concern and love and closeness—I guess because you have to band together. I don't think I would've known of that or been exposed to that had it not been for your being gay. It's been a richness beyond measure. It's wonderful. There's no downside for me at all.

Scott: Are there any big disappointments in me?

Jackie: Well, you know, if I could've made you any different, you would've been toilet trained a lot sooner. [*laughs*] I'm sorry, Scott, but that was awful! That went on forever. . . . Honestly, I'd have to think hard to come up with something else.

Scott: It's kind of funny. I think of myself as an emotional person about lots of things—like at the drop of a hat I can start crying at a movie or something like that—but for some reason, where you're concerned, I try not to be very emotional. I worry sometimes that you'll never know just how deeply I love you. And sometimes it's scary for me to imagine life without you.

Jackie: You don't let me get away with stuff—I always know that you are watching with a critical eye. But it's good that you don't let me be lazy—you don't let me give you easy answers for when I don't go to the gym. At some point, the tables turned, and now you sort of watch over and instruct me, and that's okay.

Scott: It's so funny, I don't tell you this, but I have conversations with friends about you and Dad all the time—little things that I notice, changes in you. And it's like I want to deny the fact that time is passing on. On some level I think that if I push you or if I make you work harder at things, then it'll make you stronger and you won't be able to just drift into whatever long good-night it is that people talk about—it'll be something that has to claim you. And I guess I see it as my way of making sure you're around. . . . I don't know what life will be like. It really scares me.

Jackie: That's something I can't make better for you. You're a strong guy; you've got all kinds of resources. I don't doubt it'll be tough, but you'll be okay. No question—you'll be just fine. You always have been. You and I haven't missed much. We spend a lot of time together, we really do. I treasure it—and you'll have those memories.

Scott: I love you.

Jackie: I love you, too. You're my life.

Recorded in New York, New York, on May 30, 2008.

YVETTE SALIBA, 30

interviews her father,

SY SALIBA, 66

about her mother, Pat Saliba.

Yvette Saliba: How did you meet Mom?

Sy Saliba: We met in Trinidad when she was twelve years old. I was fifteen. There was a flood, and several of us from different churches went together to help people who were in distress—help them clean their houses and salvage things. I saw this cute thing, and I said to myself, *She's nice.* I just kind of watched her from a distance, because I was always a very shy person.

We kind of knew each other on and off, and we didn't date for a long time. We really started to see each other seriously in the States just after I finished my sophomore year in college. So I was twenty-three then, and she was twenty.

Yvette: Do you remember your first date with her?

Sy: Yes—I didn't know what to do with her, so I just invited her to go to the zoo. She was very gracious. She said,

"Okay." But then, once we got in the car, she kind of gently said, "Do we really have to go to the zoo?" [*laughs*] So we never went to the zoo. We just drove around and talked, and then I took her back home. On the way—it was probably about eight o'clock—she said, "Oh, my word, I'm hungry." And then I realized I never offered to take her to eat or anything! I was really a clumsy clod in those days.

When I first said, "I love you," she asked, "Why?" I said, "I like your legs, and I like your hair, and I like your eyes." She looked at me and said, "Are you buying a car?" It was kind of like, *Go take a hike,* you know? I kind of learned later about all those things that women like.

We managed to muddle our way through. We got married in '68, in Kalamazoo, Michigan—I was twenty-six and she was twenty-three. By then we were both students at Andrews University. I had just finished my bachelor's degree, and she was working on hers, and we were poor as church mice. When we celebrated our anniversary of our first month, I took her to Schuler's Steak House, which was kind of like the ultimate eating place in Saint Joseph, Michigan. We spent all of twelve dollars. That was our entire month's grocery bill in those days—spent it all on that evening. She fretted with me on the way home how wanton and extravagant we were to do that. Guilt was a dominant theme in her life. [*laughs*] But she also really enjoyed life, so she oscillated between guilt and a joy of life, which was kind of interesting.

But you knew her, too, so what did you like about her?

Yvette: I think what I liked was her insatiable appetite for humor, that she always tried to find things that were funny in everything. She had a kind of audacious spirit about her. I remember as a little girl, we were driving back from Canada and you stopped at a gas station. A man told you that you needed to pay first, and then he took off with your money. You got back in the car, and Mom said, "What's wrong?" You said, "The man took my money!" She rolled down the window and leaned out and started to shout, "Thief, thief, thief!" [*laughs*] She was just kind of bold.

And then just how much you both would like to talk. I remember William and I talking one time about how when we would go to sleep, we would hear you guys just talking—about work, about different people in the neighborhood, and that sort of thing. Just talking *endlessly*.

Sy: Yeah, we enjoyed each other. The conversations never seemed to end. It's amazing, over the years, we never even felt like two different people, even though we were. It was like our spirits merged and we were soul mates. We just became one.

She became sick in 1997, when we were here in Orlando. The metaphor that I keep thinking of and still keep thinking of is that we were two canoes on a stream. And then there was a split, a fork in the stream. She took one stream and I took the other. And for a long time, we would paddle together. We could hold hands, even though we were in different canoes and we were set on a different course. And then gradually the streams kind of moved away, and we could no longer hold hands but we could look at each other, talk to each other. Then it got further and further away, until we just lost each other. That still stays with me to this day.

Yvette: I know as a daughter watching her go through that, she seemed to maintain a sense of optimism. Was that something she put on for her children?

Sy: No, it was who she was. As she said, she'd find her little oases—little things that she could look forward to, little trips or occasions that she could plan to get through the bone marrow transplant or the pain of a biopsy.

The thing I remember most about the final stages of her illness, which was very painful for me, was her strong desire to be remembered. She took all the slides that we'd shot over the years of our lives with you children, and she made a DVD with photos of each of us. She spent hours doing this. It was her way of trying to make sure that we don't ever forget her, that we remember her for who she was, what she did, and how she shaped our lives. That was a very painful thing—to see her struggle for memory.

But it was a great journey. You know, we didn't plan on you. Pat was just beginning a program in a master's of fine arts, because she loved to paint and she loved to sculpt. She had done a few courses and was really enthusiastic about getting back into life after having raised the boys. And then all of a sudden in the spring of 1978, she started to feel chilly. She couldn't figure out what was wrong. Then she heard the news that she was pregnant, and she was really angry with me. I was like, "Honey, why are you angry at me? Angry is out of proportion. What did I do? I had a small part to play in this." [*laughs*]

And then you were born. She dropped out of the master's program. She painted on her own, and she never took it back up. But in a sense, she sculpted her life in you. That was better than any stone or marble sculpture, because you are her handiwork.

I'll never forget her. Because whenever I look at you, I'll remember your mother.

Recorded in Orlando, Florida, on February 17, 2009.

BARBARA DUNDON, 60

talks with her husband,

JACK DUNDON, 68

about her mother, Dorothy Lang.

Barbara Dundon: The thing I'm proudest of is the five years that you and I spent with Mom—her last five years. We moved her from Florida up here to an assisted living place in Philadelphia, and we had movie night together with her every Saturday night. We'd get pizza, and we'd bring it to her little sitting room and set it all up so that it was like a special little dining room. We'd have wine: she always had white zinfandel, that god-awful sweet stuff, and we'd toast to the three of us. We'd eat the greasy pizza and watch whatever movie we had that night. You often would bring her fresh fruit from home, and I'd do her pills, and this was our routine for five years—every Saturday night. It was turning a pretty sad situation into something that transformed all three of us.

She looked forward to those Saturday nights *so much*. You knew all the little ways to tease her that would make her laugh, or to compliment her to make her feel feminine, and I just loved that you were so close with her. It didn't ever feel like a burden to you. I think you looked forward to Saturday night as much as I did.

Jack Dundon: I did! What I remember is her preference for sex and violence in the movies. [*laughs*]

Barbara: Right. She *did* like sex and violence. And her boyfriend! Oh, my gosh! What a story. She met Robert when she was ninety, and he was seventeen years her junior— remember, there weren't many able-bodied men in this assisted living place. He was a hot number there for all the women—and he chose Mom! He picked her out, he pursued her, he brought her flowers, cards—he was *hot* for Mom. And she loved it! She flourished under this love and attention. It was great to see her so atitter.

We went over Christmas Eve that year, as we always did, with pizza and wine and Christmas cookies. As we were leaving, I said, "We'll see you tomorrow, Mom. How about ten o'clock?" We all came back on Christmas Day with the presents from her grandchildren and the whole family. I mean, we always opened presents Christmas morning, and why would this be any different? So we arrived in the morning and started to open the door, but it was locked! I thought, *What's the matter?* So we knocked, and I said, "Mom, we're here!" I jiggled the doorknob; nothing happened. Finally, we heard voices in the room, and *shuffle shuffle*, I hear Mom's little walker coming toward the door: "Oh, honey, I'll be right there." [*laughs*] We walk in, and there's Robert, and he was putting his *shoes* back on. On Christmas Day! My God, it was unbelievable! [*laughs*] Robert made a hasty exit when he saw that the family was there to do Christmas. Everybody was kind of embarrassed, but we got over it.

We were there for her at the very end, holding her hand—remember that? The last Saturday night that we had together, I held her hand, and you moved over close to the bed, too, and we just talked with her—she wasn't able to talk much at that point, but she was spirited in her own way, with her face and her gestures, and she loved hearing stories.

Sunday she started to fail. Thursday morning, she died. I called you right away. We went over, and each of us kissed her and touched her skin, which was cool. We'd never been with someone who just died. It was creepy and awful and wonderful—it was *all* of those things.

Jack: What a blessing it was to be there. In a way, she had become my mother. I'd said that to her many times—that when we visited her, I felt like I was going home. It was how I was welcomed, how we knew each other, how we had cared for her. I realized after she died how much I missed having a mother. And I'll never have a mother like that again.

Recorded in New York, New York, on March 9, 2008.

Mom

CAROL KIRSCH, 59

is interviewed by her daughter,

REBECCA POSAMENTIER, 30

Carol Kirsch: My dad was always a tremendous support for me. I don't remember any time that he tried in any way to discourage me from doing something I wanted to do. I miss him a lot. But I've had a rocky relationship with my mom.

Rebecca Posamentier: I think that her raising you is very different than how you raised me, and that was a conscious decision on your part. What about your relationship with your mom made you decide that you didn't want that with your own daughter?

Carol: Mom was very insecure. She had polio as a child, and she had a limp for pretty much all her life. She was very talented at many things: she was a terrific singer, performer, and pianist. But she felt that she was not whole somehow because she had polio.

I think I've told you this before: I was afraid to have children. But I'm *so* glad I did.

Rebecca: Me too! [*laughs*] And so is Shana. I just want to say that whatever it was that made you consciously make the decisions that you did in raising Shana and myself were amazing. I just remember thinking, *I could probably tell Mom anything and she'd be okay with it*. I remember a conversation you had with me right before I went off to college. We were sitting on your bed, and you spilled the beans about how there were times that you had made mistakes and you didn't feel you could tell your parents about it, so you had to figure out how to get out of it on your own. You said that no matter what happens—even if it's horrible, even if it's terrible and I can solve it on my own—I should *still* tell you, and we'd talk about it. I felt like you were just genuinely *there,* no matter what happened.

You were always there for the good: good grades, internships, everything. That's just as important as being there when I had mono in college and went unconscious. Next thing I knew, I woke up in the hospital bed and you were there next to me. I couldn't understand how you'd gotten there so fast—but you basically hopped a plane and flew down the second you heard I was so sick. And you would do that for any of your kids. Those are the qualities of motherhood that I want to have, too.

Carol: Well, I'm not as calm and cool and collected as I used to be. [*laughs*] It's not easy. I know that there's nothing I can do about the Alzheimer's, and I know it's not my fault—

I have to live with it. I try to make the most of each day, because I'm not the kind of person who sits and wallows in self-pity.

For me, right now, what's important is to be as close to family as I can be. I just am so grateful to have all of you in my life.

Rebecca: I feel so lucky to have had such a wonderful childhood and still have your support at thirty years old and know that I'm gonna have it till I'm fifty, hopefully. It really gives me *so* much confidence going into my own motherhood for the first time. I know I'm gonna be a good mom—and I know that because I had a good mom as a role model. I had somebody who cared about me. Just like your father always supported you, you always supported me. You have those qualities, and you did a great job in passing them down. It's my dream to pass them on to my own children as well.

Sophia is not due for another seven weeks or so, but when she comes, what are some of the things that you would want to be able to pass on to her? What are some of the things that you'd want her to know?

Carol: Well, I'd want her to know that she's going to be very loved. When she's old enough, I'd like to tell her stories about my grandparents and my parents. I'm worried that my Alzheimer's will get worse and that I won't be able to spend the time I want with her. . . . I look forward to taking her places. I really hope I can do that for a while.

Rebecca: Me too. I used to love getting tucked in at night. I know that you'll do that for the baby when she's a baby. . . . [*crying*]

Carol: Oh, I will, honey.

Rebecca: I think I got tucked in till I was going off to college! But I used to love just sitting in bed and having you sing a lullaby to me. And you will for the baby, too. I just think it would be great if you could just sing a lullaby for her—for me and for her. And for future babies that aren't here, and aren't twinkling in anyone's eye quite yet, maybe you could sing one of the lullabies.

Carol: Okay. [*sings*] *Tu, lu, lu, lu, lu, hush. To, lu, lu, lu, lu, hush-a-by. Dream of the angels way up high. Tu, lu, lu, lu, lu, don't you cry. Mommy won't go away. Stay in my arms, while you still can. Childhood is but a day. To, lu, lu, lu, lu, hush-a-by. Mommy won't go away.*

Recorded in Lafayette, California, on December 13, 2007.

AFTERWORD

I was lucky enough to give StoryCorps its first-ever test run in a booth jury-rigged out of Styrofoam baffles inside a Chinatown recording studio in early 2003. For StoryCorps Interview #1, I chose to speak to my great uncle Sandy, the last survivor of my grandparents' generation.

Reserved and wry with a quiet, country-boy charm, Sandy couldn't have been any more different than his beloved late wife, my eccentric aunt Birdie, who insisted that, among other notable accomplishments, she was the inventor of fruit salad. Getting Sandy into this recording booth would answer a lot of questions I had about StoryCorps—how would an introvert take to being interviewed? Would Sandy even agree to talk? Would he feel violated by being asked personal questions about his life?

Happily, the interview worked: in forty minutes, Sandy

recounted the anti-Semitism he had faced as one of the few Jewish children in a small Connecticut town; he spoke with grace and humor about his half-century romance with my great-aunt Birdie; and he cried over the void her death had left in his life. At the end of the interview Sandy told me that the session had meant a great deal to him. Later I learned that he listened to the CD of his interview over and over again as he drove around New York City in his car. (As I write, Uncle Sandy is ninety-four and still going strong!) StoryCorps had passed a critical test, and we moved forward toward the launch of the project.

Life got very busy. I worked nonstop with a small team to get StoryCorps off the ground and to sustain it through the first challenging year. Months passed, and while I really wanted to take my own mother to the booth for a StoryCorps interview, it just felt like there wasn't the time. It took more than a year before I brought my mom to the booth for what would be my second-ever StoryCorps interview, the project's 1,013th.

As we walked into the booth to begin our conversation, I was happy to have the chance to steal an hour with my mom, but I really didn't expect to hear anything I hadn't heard before. My mom and I are quite close, and we talk all the time. Forty minutes later, though, there was barely a thing she had told me that I had known before.

Mom talked about her great-grandfather, a physician in

Vienna who went house to house caring for sick families during a typhoid epidemic in the nineteenth century. At the time visiting these quarantined homes was forbidden. One day he was caught coming out of a contaminated house and punished by having his hands chopped off and lye poured over his hands. He died soon after.

She told me about her grandfather, who owned a tiny, decidedly unsuccessful hardware store on 110th Street in Manhattan. He was, she said, a "pinpoint Talmudic scholar"—if you stuck a pin through this Jewish text and told him what word the pin hit on the first page, he could tell you precisely what word the pin would hit on each successive page. He would spend his days in his empty store, hunched over this great book he loved so dearly. Occasionally a customer would walk in and ask a question, only to be shushed: "I waited two hours for you, you can wait two minutes for me!" And then he'd finish whatever Talmud portion he was studying.

She talked about my birth: "I watched it in a mirror—it was very colorful. They put you in the little bassinette, and I leaned over and I said, 'Hello, David, this is your mom!' For months afterward, I would dream the colors of your birth that I saw in that mirror." I asked her what lessons she'd learned in life: "I've learned that when things are really bad, they're not going to stay that way. I've also learned that good breeds good—if you do good, more good will come of it. It's like light—it attracts. That's just the way it is."

It's been five years since that conversation. In that time, I've become a dad, and I've seen my mom evolve from a great mother to a terrific grandmother. It makes me happy to know that my son, my son's children, and the generations to follow will one day get to know my mother, Jane Isay, through the StoryCorps interview we recorded that December day.

If there's a single piece of advice I can offer six years into this work it's this: *Don't wait.* Take the time to show the people important to you that you love them by interviewing them about their lives. A few years ago, I had an appointment with my sports medicine doctor, who ran a practice with his dad. He told me that his father was retiring, I told him he needed to take his dad to a StoryCorps booth. He promised he would. It was my last appointment with him. Last week, a StoryCorps intern was riding the subway, reading our first book, *Listening Is an Act of Love,* when this doctor tapped her on the shoulder and told her he knew me. When the young woman told him she worked at StoryCorps, he said: "Just tell Dave this: I waited too long."

Every day I hear from people who meant to record a beloved relative or friend but waited too long. I hope after reading *Mom* you'll be inspired to honor someone important in your life by recording an interview—either at one of our StoryCorps facilities or by using your own recording equipment. (You can find all sorts of helpful resources at www .storycorps.org).

I also hope you'll spread the word about our efforts. We want to encourage the entire nation to take the time to ask life's important questions of a loved one—or even a stranger—and *really* listen to the answers. We hope to shower this country with more of the sorts of stories you've just read—authentic voices that remind us what's truly important, that tell real American stories, and that show us all the possibilities life presents when lived to its fullest.

I hope you'll join us as we work to weave StoryCorps into the fabric of American life and into the lives of all Americans. Onward!

—Dave Isay, October 2009

ACKNOWLEDGMENTS

This book owes its existence to the remarkable curatorial eye, deft editing skills, and disciplined project management of Lizzie Jacobs, StoryCorps's editor. Lizzie was assisted with diligence by Isaac Kestenbaum. Thanks also to this book's readers, all of them mothers, who weighed in on numerous versions of the manuscript on tight deadlines: Kathrina Proscia; Eve Claxton; my wife, Jennifer Gonnerman; and my mom, Jane Isay. Gratitude to Darren Reidy, the Tape Transcription Center, Jennifer Kotter, Emma Tsui, and Jordan Sayle.

Thanks to Scott Moyers for his steadfast support and wise counsel. Thanks also to our remarkable, ever-vigilant agent, David Black, whose loyalty, attention, and heart never cease to amaze. At Penguin Press thanks to Lindsay Whalen, Liz Calamari, Tracy Locke, Stephen Morrison, and our editor and publisher, Ann Godoff, the best in the business.

ACKNOWLEDGMENTS

Thanks to all of our supporters, with special thanks to our lead funders: Patricia DeStacy Harrison; Gara LaMarche; Larry Kaplen; Joe and Carol Reich for our Memory Loss Project; and Stan Shuman, Deborah Leff, and the StoryCorps Board. Thanks also to Peggy Bulger and the American Folklife Center at the Library of Congress. Thanks to the inimitable Ellen McDonnell, Ellen Weiss, Dana Davis Rehm, and everyone else at NPR who has a hand in our weekly broadcasts on *Morning Edition*.

Most of all, thanks to the entire tireless StoryCorps team— the most brilliant and committed group of people anyone could ever hope to work with.

FAVORITE STORYCORPS
QUESTIONS

- What was the happiest moment of your life? The saddest?
- Who was the most important person in your life? Can you tell me about him or her?
- Who has been the kindest to you in your life?
- What are the most important lessons you've learned in life?
- What is your earliest memory?
- Are there any words of wisdom you'd like to pass along?
- What are you proudest of in your life?
- How has your life been different from what you'd imagined?
- How would you like to be remembered?
- Do you have any regrets?

- What does your future hold?
- Is there anything that you've never told me but want to tell me now?
- Is there something about me that you've always wanted to know but have never asked?

CONTINUE THE CONVERSATION

Visit www.storycorps.org to

- learn how to interview someone important to you;
- listen to more stories and share them with others;
- subscribe to our podcast;
- find out where our booths are located and how to bring StoryCorps to your community;
- support StoryCorps;
- read about the National Day of Listening.

One hundred percent of the royalties from this book will be donated to StoryCorps, a not-for-profit organization.

Lead funding for StoryCorps comes from the Corporation for Public Broadcasting.

Other major 2009 funders include: the Atlantic Philanthropies, anonymous, the Kaplen Foundation, Joe and Carol Reich, the Lower Manhattan Development Corporation, and NPR.

Additional funders include the Ford Foundation, the Annenberg Foundation, the Carnegie Corporation, the Marc Haas Foundation, the Charina Endowment Fund, Bloomberg L.P., the Fetzer Institute, the National Endowment for the Arts, the Open Society Institute, and the BayTree Fund.

Legal services are generously donated by Latham & Watkins and Holland & Knight.

For a complete and current list of all of our supporters, please visit our Web site: www.storycorps.org.

National Partners:

ABOUT THE AUTHOR

Dave Isay is the founder of StoryCorps and the recipient of numerous broadcasting honors, including five Peabody Awards and a MacArthur "genius" fellowship. He is the author/editor of four books that grew out of his public radio documentary work, including the first StoryCorps book, *Listening Is an Act of Love*, a *New York Times* bestseller.